GOD'S PATH FROM
BONDAGE TO FREEDOM

DELIVER US FROM EVIL

W. Charles Greenfield

Master Press
8905 Kingston Pike Suite 12-316
Knoxville, TN 37923

Deliver Us From Evil
© Copyright 2003

Published by Master Press
8905 Kingston Pike Suite 12-316, Knoxville, TN 37923
Master Press website: www.master-press.com
1-800-325-9136

Distributed by Master Press

ISBN 0-9646543-7-7
All Rights Reserved.

No part of this book may be reproduced or transmitted in any form or by any means, electronic, mechanical, including photocopying, recording, or by any information storage and retrieval system, without permission in writing from the publisher.

Printed in the United States of America.

This book is dedicated with thanks to our Messianic Jewish brothers and sisters whose welcomed presence in the Body of Christ is bringing restoration to the ruined and desolate cities.

All direct Bible quotations are taken from the King James Version.

Contents

Introduction: 7

Chapter 1: Basic Understandings That Begin the Journey 11

Chapter 2: Purification: Getting Rid of Impurities 29

Chapter 3: The Night of Deliverance 43

Chapter 4: Deliverance: Breaking the Yoke 61

Chapter 5: The Road to Redemption 71

Chapter 6: Redemption: A Change of Ownership 83

Chapter 7: Praise 99

Chapter 8: Welcome to the Wilderness 111

Introduction

All too many Christians hear the word of the Lord week after week. They have regular contact with other believers and know the ways of God. Many of these individuals have been touched, often by the power and presence of God. Yet, amazingly, their lives continue unchanged. There is little relief from their burdens, little freedom into the life of God. An intimate relationship with the Lord seems out of their grasp. Evil appears to have the upper hand, and oppression in their lives is the norm rather than the exception. How can this be? How can trouble abound in the lives of those who have been ordained to rule over evil? How can those who should be leading in strength be led by their weakness? Yet these people continue in bondage while God brings dramatic freedom to others.

Throughout history, God has been bringing radical deliverances to His people. Without subscription to any plan, without the permission of men, He has been supernaturally rebuking evil and bringing freedom to hopeless lives. These supernatural acts may seem random. While some people are delivered others remain bound. Yet God is not cruel. He does have a path leading to freedom available to anyone who will call on Him. Anyone drawing breath on this planet can be freed from evil. Today, every person can experience the wonder of living free in an intimate relationship with the living God. They can walk the path to the "Promised Land."

Today, we are seeing God's path to freedom come alive before our eyes. Yet it is not a new path at all. In actuality, it was presented to us in great detail a long time ago. It is a path that has its roots deep in Jewish tradition, having been outlined extensively in Scripture, so that we can understand it and live in it. It is in the Passover Seder that this path is revealed, and through the Seder, God intends it to be remembered until time itself ends.

During the Jewish Passover celebration four cups of wine, consumed at differing points in the meal, distinguish four specific actions that God accomplished in freeing Israel in Egypt. The Lord Jesus Himself emphasized these cups at the "Last Supper." These four cups are: Purification (known in Jewish circles as "sanctification"), Deliverance, Redemption, and Praise. As we come to understand these cups we begin to realize that collectively they outline our path to total and complete freedom in God. The Passover (as celebrated for thousands of years) is our visible reminder of the overwhelming goodness of our Lord and His faithfulness to deliver us from evil.

The Passover celebration tells the story of God reclaiming His people. The starting point for this reclamation was a restoration of His Lordship in their lives. The same is true for us today. Once "Lordship" has been established in the heart, God begins a process that brings us from bondage to freedom. Regardless of the evil at hand, the road to freedom is the same for each one of us individually and corporately. God's method for bringing us out of the shadow of death into His life is the same whether facing an evil dictator, a world-renowned terrorist, a strong principality, an abusive spouse, a corrupt business partner, a wayward child, a foul tongue, or an unforgiving heart. Lordship is the starting point. Without Jesus being Lord of a person's life, there is no tenacity, trust, or desire to endure the course to liberty ordained by God.

This book lays out God's plan of freedom for those who will submit to Him. It demonstrates an all-powerful God who is intimately involved in the lives of His people. You will see an awesome, incredibly wise and caring God who, through His Son, placed evil in its proper perspective by delivering us from it. Through this powerful and incredible work, He has bought us back as His own so that we now have a pure song of praise on our lips.

It is my hope that as you read this book you will be able to identify where God is working in your own life. I believe that as the truth of the Passover Seder and the four cups of wine dawns on you, it will begin to create in you a desire for God's best, for yourself as well as for others. It will give you hope in your current situation. Then you will be drawn into praise as He reveals His majesty and you learn how to trust Him in all situations with all your heart. It is my prayer that, as you read, you will be amazed at the wonder of the Lord Jesus Christ (just like the disciples of old).

Years ago, the disciples of Jesus watched in wonder as our Lord lived with and among them. They witnessed that which no man had ever seen - One who lived in an intimate and personal relationship with the living God. Previous to the coming of Jesus they knew God as the Creator, but He remained aloof and far removed from them. For them, God could be obeyed but certainly never touched. However, when Jesus came and lived His life among them He conversed with the God of Abraham, Isaac, and Jacob as a son conversed with a father. They had previously known Him as Elohim, the all-powerful One, but not as Father. Yet as they observed Jesus interacting with His Father during His earthly ministry, they understood the significance of the truth that Jesus was God's Son. That interaction and that revelation were revolutionary for the disciples.

While they had previously learned how to pray, it was while watching the Lord converse with His Father that they realized how much they had to learn about real communion with God. Confused and undoubtedly in turmoil, they approached the Lord requesting that He teach them to pray. Luke records His simple, yet astounding response:

> *"Our Father which art in heaven, hallowed be Thy name. Thy kingdom come. Thy will be done on earth as it is in heaven. Give us this day our daily bread. And forgive us our debts, as we forgive our debtors. And lead us not into temptation, but deliver us from evil, for Thine is the kingdom and the power and the glory forever. Amen." (Luke 11:2-4)*

While many books have been written on this short prayer (and no doubt will continue to be) the following pages are dedicated to the succinct plea found towards the end of the Lord's Prayer, "Deliver Us from

Evil." Within that important phrase will be found all that God has for His people in regards to deliverance from the power of evil. In order to understand it though, we will have to answer many questions along the way such as "What is evil?" and, "How do we become entrapped by it?" We will also need to know how we are delivered from evil so that its effects are removed from our lives. And more importantly we must answer the questions "What is God's pattern for deliverance?" and "What role (if any) do we play in God's process to freedom?"

In order to answer these and other questions we will of course have to know exactly what is meant by the term deliverance and whether or not it is the end of the road to freedom or just a step along the journey. This will help us to know what we can expect along the way and what barriers stand between our freedom and us. Using the backdrop of the biblical account of the Exodus from Egypt as well as Jewish traditions surrounding the Passover Seder, these are some of the questions to be addressed in this book. I also draw heavily from real life experiences found in the Body of Jesus Christ.

In teaching us to pray for our deliverance, the Lord demonstrates His desire to free us from the influence and burden of evil. He bids us to ask Him for it because He truly wants to bring us deliverance. God wants us to be free. He wants us to fulfill our destiny here on earth. Therefore, deliverance from evil of every kind is something we can ask for in the confidence that God will grant our request. This boldness comes from asking in accordance with His will (I John 5:14-15). God wants us to be delivered from evil! Deliverance belongs to us as children of God! Yes, freedom is available to anyone who honestly calls the Son of God, "Lord!"

So, strap yourself in. Lets begin this journey from bondage to freedom, from evil to glory, from trouble to peace, from oppression to praise, and from slavery to inheritance!

CHAPTER 1

Basic Understandings that Begin the Journey

> *"For as the heavens are higher than the earth, so are My ways higher than your ways, and My thoughts than your thoughts."* Isaiah 55:9

The Christian life is a growing process that brings us from "faith to faith" and "glory to glory" (Romans 1:17, 2 Corinthians 3:18). We are continually being changed and challenged. As we grow, we find our ways of conduct and our very thought patterns changing. What we thought was critically important ten years ago we may not give a second thought to today. The ways in which we once handled problems are changed as our priorities change. The way we conduct ourselves in our relationships changes as God replaces our heart of stone with a heart of flesh. We begin to think with a heavenly mindset - one diametrically opposed to the prevailing thought patterns around us.

We should not be surprised to find that our prevailing thoughts regarding our relationship with God and our life in Him fall short of His perspective on the subjects. When we make God's way of thinking in these matters our own, freedom from evil will flow naturally. In contrast, when our perspective on these issues is worldly rather than godly, we create barriers that hinder us from understanding God's purpose for our deliverance and enjoying the freedom of the children of God.

The rest of this chapter will address many of the barriers created by improper thought patterns. We will look at God versus evil, the reality of God's cleaning process (for those of us who are being saved), and the pattern of sin and death. Once these areas have been given proper perspective, the journey will begin. God's pattern for deliverance and freedom will begin to unfold.

God versus Evil

"Why can't I seem to get past the same troubles?" "Why am I always fighting the same demons?" "If Christ accomplished all at Calvary, why do I still struggle?" "I thought I was delivered from that stronghold. Why is it back?" "If the Lord's burden is light, why do I feel so heavy?" "How could God allow this to happen?" "Where is the reality of a personal relationship with God?"

The issues at the heart of these questions all stem from one source; evil in and around our lives. Today most of God's people have little understanding of how God views evil or His plan of freedom from it. As a result, far too many of us are living our lives under the burden of evil. The thing that we were created to dominate controls us instead. Forces that we were designed to conquer rule us. We accept evil as a natural part of life. In fact, many lay the effects of evil at the Lord's feet, believing that He brought the evil into their lives. Some people actually believe that God sits in heaven and dishes out evil on a whim. Holding this view results in their believing that it is God who has placed sin in their lives. Some even go as far as to thank God for allowing them to pay the price for sin.

Yet God has nothing to do with evil. It is true that He may use evil for his own purpose, but He will never tempt us with evil. That is because evil is not a part of God or His kingdom. Understanding the nature of evil, as well as our relationship to evil, is key to seeing the hand of God bring freedom into our lives. If we understand what evil is and that it has no place in our lives we can, therefore, ask God for deliverance from it.

We have already seen how the Lord Jesus taught his disciples to pray, "deliver us from evil." He would not have taught them to pray that way unless He wanted them to be free from evil. There was something better than living under the influence of evil. There was relief from the weight of evil if they would simply ask for it! There was a way to get past all of those troubles that continually plagued them. They could have final victory over demons. Their struggles could end because freedom was available. God is the God of deliverance and He desired to be that in their lives.

This is God's will for us today as well. God desires to be just as much a God of deliverance for us as He was for them. Yet He is not merely interested in our freedom from evil, but in our being focused on the marvel and glory of who He is. His desire is not that we merely be freed from something but that we are freed from evil to focus on Him! We are to be tied to Him; literally "living in Him." God's interest in our lives is not focused solely on our relationship with evil, but that we begin to live as He lives. His nature is to become our nature, His thoughts to become our thoughts. God wants His way of existence to become our very way of life!

If God wants us to live as He lives and have His thoughts, then understanding who God is and how He lives is very important. Who is this God who has called us to be His own? How does He live? Answering these questions will undoubtedly consume the fullness of eternity. Yet through the Scriptures and our own walk with the Lord, we can catch a glimpse of God's reality and therefore understand how He would have us to live.

We begin by contemplating who God is. For it is only when we come to know Him in reality that we can begin to understand how He wants us to live. We must start with the fact that God is a holy God, which in its simplest form means that He is pure. That means that there is nothing wrong with God; everything about God is good and right. Scripture reveals that He is not only righteous, but also majestic, and all-powerful. Not only is there nothing bad in Him, but it is also true that He has no limitations. He doesn't make mistakes. Everything He does is done properly. He created all things, which means that all creation is subject to His authority. He is also a God of order and completeness.

So to state it simply, there is nothing lacking in God. Problems do not exist with Him. There are no disturbances, distresses, or pains that plague God. He never wakes up thinking to Himself, "I wish I hadn't done that last night." Nothing takes God by surprise. He never has to wonder what to do next since He knows the end from the beginning. Nothing, therefore, ever throws God for a loop.

What is the result of this? It is that evil cannot exist in or around God. In heaven there is no such thing as evil. God is absolutely free from any form of evil.

What exactly is evil? Often, when we speak about evil, we relegate it the realm of the mysterious or vile. We think of evil as those things that are hideous or disgusting, such as witchcraft, pagan sacrifices, inappropriate sexual behavior, etc. Or we consider things that are really shocking as evil. Yet when we come to Scripture we discover that God's view of evil is much broader than this.

A study of the original language of the words translated in the Bible as "evil," reveals the heavenly view of evil to be much different than our common views. What we would brush off as a nuisance God often calls evil. For example, He views trouble as evil. Chaos, problems, and disturbances are also often viewed as evil, not to mention injustice, corruption, lack of integrity, prejudice, rejection, anger, perversion, manipulation, and pride. In other words, anything that stands against the order, rule, or completeness of God is evil. A person who causes trouble is often called, "wicked" in Scripture. Therefore a person who is a troublemaker is farthest from the heart of God. That's because a troublemaker not only rebels against God personally, he or she leads others away from God as well, causing trouble for those who wish to remain faithful.

Evil (trouble) stands against the very nature of who God is and therefore cannot co-exist with Him. God is completely intolerant of evil. He does not coddle it in any way. He doesn't have a sliding scale for evil. God doesn't look at one form as better or worse than another. Evil has no place in the domain of God. And God expects His view of evil to be ours as well! In this age where "intolerance" is a four-letter word, God expects us to disdain anything that causes trouble in our lives. We are to be people of integrity in whose presence evil cannot exist. He wants us to live as He lives and that means free from trouble. Any trouble that does enter our lives is to be brought to God's attention or immediately dealt with. When trouble builds to a point beyond our own control God expects us to cry out, "Deliver us from Evil!"

And that is the good news. God always provides a way out when evil approaches us. Our responsibility is to take it and be freed from evil. God expects nothing less of us. Can you imagine the people of Israel telling God "No thank you," when He offered them deliverance them from bondage? Or the Apostle Paul saying, "Thanks, but no thanks," when the risen Lord appeared to Him on his way to Damascus? Instead of swimming to the Lord that morning on the beach following the resurrection, could you imagine Peter running and hiding? Such an idea is silly. Yet many of us are daily saying "No" to His offer of deliverance, choosing instead to embrace rejection, depression, guilt, lust, perversion, etc. We accept evil as a natural part of our lives. When God offers His deliverance we turn Him down for any number of reasons. We say "No" to God often without even realizing it. In the courts of heaven, saying, "No" to God is unheard of and it should be here on this earth as well. Regardless of how we feel, saying "Yes" to God's deliverance should be the norm for our lives.

Our heart and motivation should be the same as our Lord's when He walked the earth—to be pleasing to the Father. When God tells us that He wants to be our deliverance and strength, our response must be "Yes." Regardless of our own situations or feelings, we are expected to submit to His word because we love Him and wish to be pleasing to Him. Our heart becomes like John the Baptist who declared, "I must decrease that He may increase." Our heart and motivation then turns heavenward. Our focus turns away from ourselves and becomes fixed on God. Our desires become His desires. We become purposeful in attempting to determine how to best please God, looking for ways to bring Him the glory due His Name. We look forward to being under His control. We submit to Him! And when we do, God is able to begin His work in us.

We often think of submission as a nasty thing but the truth is, submitting to God is not difficult. Perhaps we carry a wrong view of submission because we associate it with a tyrannical authority structure. For some, the word submit conjures up pictures of a chauvinistic husband misusing his wife. Yet submission simply means, "to give place." We submit when we yield our rights to another person. When we submit to another we are giving them a place in our lives as well as a right to give us input. We are yielding the right-of-way to another person. Likewise, when we submit to God we are giving Him a place in our lives - the right to have input in our lives. We are yielding our own rights to Him. When we do submit to God, He transforms us completely. Through submission, God begins removing evil and its effects from our lives.

The way in which God brings His people out of evil and into freedom is totally amazing. He brings us through a process which conforms us to His own image. This process often defies any human logic. Those who have experienced this process are often unable to find words to adequately describe what they have witnessed. Words like "awesome", "miraculous", and "overwhelming" are often used, yet even these superlatives fall short of describing God's work of deliverance. That's because words cannot begin to express what God does in the lives of His people. God's process of taking people from evil to freedom leads them down roads they never would have chosen themselves. For example, instead of making them strong, God makes them vulnerable. Instead of action, He often produces inaction. Instead of one instant victory, a person must endure a series of battles that may seem overwhelming at the time. Instead of success, He often allows failure. Instead of prosperity, there is often poverty. Instead of moving safely north to the Promised Land, He causes them to travel south to a dead end peninsula. Regardless of the journey, the wonderful destination He brings us to could not have been comprehended. Only God could have accomplished what the journey has produced. Only God could have conquered such overwhelming odds.

The Bible is full of examples of God's remarkable deliverance and freedom. Abraham, Isaac, Jacob, Moses, Joshua, David, Nehemiah, Esther, Jeremiah, Daniel, Zerubbabel, Joseph, Peter, and Paul begin the list of names given to us who have experienced, and serve as examples of, God's pattern for deliverance. The pattern God has established to bring His people from evil to freedom is the same today as it has been throughout the course of history. Freedom from evil is available to us just as it was for those who have gone before us.

The pattern God uses for our deliverance has been succinctly chronicled in the historical account of the children of Israel's exodus from Egypt and has been permanently affixed to our remembrance in the Passover celebration. God's pattern for deliverance may be read by anyone who would like to read the first fifteen chapters of the Book of Exodus. It may also be seen annually in Jewish households worldwide as the Passover is celebrated as it has been for thousands of years. The pattern is seen in the Jewish Passover's four cups. Like the four Passover cups God's pattern for deliverance has four stages. Four distinct steps outline this process to freedom. They are:

> *Purification (In Jewish circles called Sanctification or Holiness)*
> *Deliverance*
> *Redemption*
> *Praise*

Understanding the depths of this pattern will provide security in the midst of change. While the world constantly changes around us, we know that God is in control and doing something special on our behalf. In addition, an understanding of what God is doing provides trust which will lead to faith, and faith keeps fear from short-circuiting the process. This is a process which no human being can take credit for. It is ordained by God with very little action required by us. And it is not limited to the rebuking of evil. It is a process focused on the freedom of God's people, more interested in the heart of the person than the evil currently overpowering them.

In the following chapters we will look carefully at each of these cups of wine to understand God's pattern of deliverance. Before we can understand it though, it is important that we realize what happened when you and I accepted God's gift of His Son Jesus Christ. It began a process by which we are being saved from ourselves, demonic forces, and the world system in which we live. As we understand this, life becomes easier. For those who are being saved God is at work to free them from the evil in these three realms. The good news is that He is in control of the process, so I don't have to be! He can be fully trusted so that I can accept who I am, with the hope of who I will be at the end of the process.

"For those of us being saved"
I Corinthians 1:18

Deliverance and freedom can only come from one source. That source deals with the root problem and removes the evil that is causing the trouble. That source will take us off the path of death and destruction and place us on a path leading to His life. That source will treat the true disease and remove the individual symptoms at the same time. That source is God! Deliverance and freedom can only be found in Him. When He delivers, it is finished. When the process is complete, there is no trouble and a new life is enjoyed.

Freedom will never be found outside of God, therefore we are completely dependent on Him. Realizing this dependence is, in fact, the first step in our deliverance from evil. That does not mean that we may not turn to other people to walk with us in the process. Yet we must see that God is our only hope for deliverance. We must come to a place where we are desperate to have God move in our lives!

God designed us to be dependent on Him. When we are in trouble He wants us to turn to Him; in fact, He expects us to turn to Him. He has placed within every human being a heart felt longing that searches for Him. He wants to be our total source in life. God is so jealous of this role in our lives that He will not allow anything or anyone to interfere. We cannot fill the void that God has designed into us for Himself with anything except Him. We may attempt to fill the void with something or someone else. We may try to handle our own battles. We may attempt to battle evil on our own. However we will never find peace or success by doing it on our own. Neither will any religious substitute fill that void. Nothing will satisfy apart from Him.

The Lord offers so much more than anything we could achieve or absorb apart from Him. He takes everything that we are and shapes, molds, removes, and plants it for His glory. Talk about holistic medicine! God deals with every aspect of who we are: spirit, soul, and body. When God has charge of a life, He cleanses, heals, and fortifies. Ways of thinking are changed. Humility and dependence are increased. In addition, God takes the evil that would destroy us and gives us the power to rule over it:

> *"For the weapons of our warfare are not carnal, but mighty through God to the pulling down of strongholds; Casting down imaginations, and every high thing that exalteth itself against the knowledge of God, and bringing into captivity every thought to the obedience of Christ; And having in a readiness to revenge all disobedience, when your obedience is fulfilled."* 2 Corinthians 10:4-6

> *"...yet I would have you wise unto that which is good, and simple concerning evil. And the God of peace shall bruise Satan under your feet shortly..."* Romans 16:19-20

> *"To the intent that now unto the principalities and powers in heavenly places might be known by the church the manifold wisdom of God,"* Ephesians 3:10

These Scriptures reveal that when God works in the life of a saint, evil no longer calls the shots. The person is no longer subject to the whims of evil, but, rather, rules over evil. Where there was previously fear caused by evil it is now vanquished. This is amazing! A short-lived, relatively insignificant human (with a life span averaging from seventy to eighty years) is found commanding forces that have existed for thousands of years. The "manifold wisdom of God is being made known, by the church, to principalities and powers in heavenly places." God has entrusted insignificant people with heavenly authority to rule over spirit beings.

In the lives of the people of God, evil becomes a tool in God's hand. The evil that has entered our life, either by our own actions or the actions of others, is used to bring His glory into our lives. Death gives way to life as the goodness of God unfolds. The forces that try to rule a life end up serving that life!

In reality, we all have areas in our life that need to be dealt with by God. Each one of us is a work in process. We all have bonds to be broken and new freedoms to come into. When one aspect of our life is brought into alignment with God's Word another aspect of our life is brought under His scrutiny. The process begins on the day we bow our knee to the Lord Jesus and the sovereignty of God the Father, and ends the day we cross through the veil and take our place in heaven.

During our life on this earth God rebukes evil on our behalf so that its hold on our life is systematically reduced. Yet that is not all that He does. He replaces that aspect of our lives which was controlled (or owned) by evil and fills the newly created void with an aspect of His own nature. When we are saved from hell, God places His love within us. When God delivers from rejection He fills with His acceptance in the beloved. When God delivers from fear He fills with His peace. Sorrow is replaced with joy. This is exactly what being brought from "faith to faith" and "glory to glory" is all about. It is this understanding that motivated many of the New Testament writers to challenge us to look forward to (as well as enjoy) adversity and trials.

Most New Testament writers looked forward to God's rebuking of evil in their lives as something to be enjoyed and anticipated. Rather than

Chapter 1

seeing a fiery trial, our forefathers saw an opportunity to have another aspect of God's nature placed within them. We can easily take this same attitude in our own lives. When evil in our life is brought to our attention we can (and should) be excited to see God placing another piece of His mind and nature within us. We look back over a history with God and see Him transforming us into His own image. We see His nature replacing our own nature. We begin to realize that though we are saved, we are, in fact, being saved!

The first question, therefore, that those of us being saved need to ask is, "Are we walking in freedom or not?" This question would appear to have an easy answer, but, unfortunately for many, that isn't the case. Many Christians are living unaware of God's freedom and, therefore, never ask for His help. They live by what they see, rather than what God declares. Instead of asking God to heal them, they ask God to be with the doctors. They have seldom, if ever, seen God heal. Or they ask God to bless their plans, rather than submitting to His plans. In this way they are much like an animal that has been raised in a zoo which has no concept of freedom. He will never dare cross the threshold of an open cage door.

Yet God has given us a weapon that blows cages wide open. It is the word of our testimony. Sharing what God has done (the word of our testimony) is extremely critical in defeating evil. If God healed you, He can heal me. If God bailed you out, He can bail me out. If God saved you, He can save me. If you can hear from God, so can I. We begin to look outside our cages and set our hopes on something outside of the current box we call our life. We begin to look for something more than what we see or are living in.

Every major change in my own life has been the result of someone sharing an aspect of his or her relationship to God with me. In addition, I have yet to see anyone escape the bounds of their own perceptions of God without someone sharing a testimony of God's work in their life. In fact, the first time God brought His deliverance in my life was the result of a single person's testimony. I once spent an entire week listening to a man share stories regarding his relationship with God and the incredible intimacy with the Holy Spirit he enjoyed. I could not believe what I was hearing as the stories kept coming all week long. Each story not only made sense, but also lined up with what I had read in Scripture. By the end of the week, I was all out of sorts and my entire life was turned upside down. I realized that I not only wanted what he had, I desperately needed it!

I appeared to have it all together on the outside yet I was rotting on the inside. I couldn't play the game anymore. I knew that my relationships had to change; with God, my wife, my children, the church and everyone else. My life depended on getting what this man had. I could not continue the way I was going. Change had to come or I would shrivel up and die. Yet as he talked hope began to build. When the man spoke it was as if God Himself was telling me, "This is what you need. You can have this too!" Things could change. In fact, things did change before the week was finished.

Another simple question we must ask is, "Do I really want to be free?" Astoundingly, many who know that God is able to free them refuse it when it is offered to them. All too many times the Lord has been at someone's door with healing, deliverance, or freedom in His hands and He has been turned away. These individuals choose to embrace evil for a variety of self-centered motives. Pride is one of the main reasons that we embrace evil. Often pride manifests itself as self-pity: "I have such a hard life; everyone feel sorry for me!" When we make statements like these our pride is being manifested, and pride keeps us from God. One of the things we easily forget is that our experiences are not unique at all. Many people have lived like we have and been treated like us. We may feel like we are undergoing something totally unique, but it is simply not true.

One evening I received a phone call from a person asking me to join a group of well meaning Christians engaged with attempting to help a woman with obvious demonic problems. When I arrived, I learned that the woman had been a practicing witch, which explained the presence of the demonic. After a prolonged period of time dealing with the demons, I asked the woman, "Where do you see yourself in a year?" Her response was immediate, "I will either be delivered or dead!" I asked her, "Which do you prefer?" The woman actually took a long time to think about it. She then replied, "Delivered, I guess." Needless to say, this woman did not want God to move on her behalf. She wasn't driven to the Lord and desperate for His moving on her account. She was more interested in the attention she was receiving from the Christians who would listen to her.

Some people actually prefer misery to freedom. They are used to trouble (evil) and may actually like having problems. Misery creates a world of its own and will share its throne with no one. Misery becomes a self-centered root that drives to the very core of a person. If people really understood the price they are paying for being self-centered they would be shocked.

So we must start by recognizing that evil is trouble, and that God has designed for me to be free. We must get to the place where we say, "Trouble is not good! We must not only want to rid our lives of trouble, we must also be willing to ask ourselves, "Are we free?" If the answer is 'No' then we must ask the obvious question; "Do we really want to be free?" To that we must answer a resounding 'Yes.'

God Save Me Please! Hosanna!

Lust, Sin, Death:
The Cycle of Destruction

"Let no man say when he is tempted, I am tempted by God: for God cannot be tempted nor tempteth He any man: but every man is tempted when he is drawn away of his own lusts and enticed. Then when lust hath conceived, it bringeth forth sin: and sin when it is finished bringeth forth death."
James 1:13-15

"For all that is in the world, the lust of the flesh, and the lust of the eyes, and the pride of life, is not of the Father, but is of the world." *I John 2:16*

Lust, sin, death, is a cycle that has plagued mankind since the Garden of Eden. Ever since the fall of Adam and Eve, we have been subject to our own destruction. The source of evil in the world and in our lives can be traced to this one origin: misguided desire. Problems, trouble, and evil all find the same root cause whether they are our own desires, the desire of another person, or even those of a group of people. Regardless of the evil at hand, self-centered desire is always found at the heart. An evil government, a corrupt culture, an oppressed town, a stymied church, a ruthless church administration committee, a nonfunctional mother, a depressed father, a hopeless child all are paying for attitudes and actions that are against the will and ways of God. Self-centeredness rather than God-centeredness comes with a price and always begins with someone entertaining his or her own desires.

The lust of the flesh, lust of the eyes, and the pride of life are at the center of every problem conceived on this earth. Every fight with evil begins with one of these three desires. Embracing self-centered desire starts the person down a path for which they will pay a hefty price. The price will be extracted. Desire embraced will exact its cost. In fact, generations to follow may have to pay for their choice of paths. Even though we like to think of ourselves as individuals we are, whether we admit it or not, tied to each other. What Dad does affects Mom and the children. What Grandma did, can have an affect on her grandchildren long after her death. How a brother behaves at school can affect how schoolteachers and staff treat other siblings. How deacon Dan conducts himself around singer Carol can determine the future of a church.

When we yield to our own desires we are yielding to temptation. The moment we do, we have gone off course and are traveling a path we should not be on. Initially everything may seem to feel so right. It is quite effortless to figure out our new direction. It is easy to persuade ourselves that this new path is God's will for us. Yet the truth is, we are deceived. What feels like the right path is in fact the fruit of a deceived heart and mind and we will end up paying for it in the long run.

Christians often use a number of excuses to justify yielding to their own desires. The following are just a few examples of some of them that

I have heard over the years:

"Pastor! Do you know what that woman said about me? I refuse to have any kind of relationship with her!"

"Do you know what my wife did? From now on, I am treating her like one of the children"

"My husband needs to change NOW or I am making a change!"

"I don't care what is right! I am tired of my wife and I want someone new."

"You know, we just had to have groceries. So, I wrote a bad check for them!"

"So what if I spent the rent money! I been under a lot of stress and deserved to get drunk."

"My husband refuses to be the spiritual leader in our house! So I am taking the role."

"My wife is great! I just like pornography. I really can't control myself!"

"I don't have to do what my parents say! They don't know what they are talking about."

"The woman at the office treats me a lot better than my wife."

"So what if I have a problem with anger! It is a family curse. It is who I am."

"The girls and I just went to check out the male strippers. Don't worry, nothing will come of it!"

Those offering these excuses really believe what they are saying. At the time, what they are saying feels and looks right. Their excuses really seem to make sense. However, their language betrays the fact that they have been deceived. They have been enticed by their own desire. While it is true that they may have been influenced by demons, they were set on following through with their actions until they got what they wanted. They had a strong desire for a certain thing, for a long time, and they were predisposed to seeking after it.

Every one of us must deal with our own self-centered desires. Because these desires look so right we must be on guard against them moment by moment. These lusts entice (tempt) and pull us away towards a path we shouldn't travel. Tempted by them, we act because we want see our desired fulfilled. Deep down they appeal to what we really want. Yet there is another part of us screaming to heaven that something isn't right. In our hearts a war rages between our flesh and spirit.

Flesh and self-centered desires are grotesque and ugly. Yet seeing our own desires (flesh) come to the surface is a normal part of every Christian's walk. Seeing the ugliness in others or ourselves should not shock us. In fact, allowing flesh to rise to the surface is a part of God's plan to bring us freedom. In our church we have a saying whenever a person gets a glimpse of his or her flesh: "Welcome to the frying pan!" We know enough not to judge the person because we know that each one of us will have our turn in the frying pan. We are not shocked by what we see because many of us have been there. Those of us who haven't will get their chance some day.

Yet there is a profound difference between seeing the flesh and our own desires, and acting out those desires. Seeing our own self-centered desires (flesh) is a normal part of living the Christian life. In fact, God commands us not to hide ourselves from our own flesh (Isaiah 58:7). That's because He wants us to be aware of our own nature and propensity to rebel against Him. Yet God never expects that we should act on these desires - in fact, to do so is wrong! Regardless of how we feel or see things, our actions must always be based on the will of God. If we do the will of God, we will stay near to Him. (In fact, the Apostle John goes a step further. John says, "He who does the will of the Father abides forever." (1 John 2:17)) If we stay near to Him, He will handle our desires for us.

What happens both spiritually and physically when we embrace our own desires? The lights begin to turn off. Praying seems more difficult. The leading of God in our lives seems further away. A vibrant relationship with God becomes more cerebral. We may blame the problem on demons to justify ourselves, yet the truth is we are losing our ability to see and sadly, may not even miss it! We are slipping into the "Valley of the Shadow of Death", which is not a physical death, but a death-like state where the dimming of the light of life takes place. Here in the shadow of death, sin begins to extract its price and we may not even be aware of it. Slowly we begin to drift asleep, becoming numbed to the things of God. It is a sleep that will prevent us from knowing the full impact of our actions until it is too late.

The behavior of a person spiraling towards destruction may be visibly observed. As death fastens its hold on an individual, it changes the way they interact with everything and everyone around them. A person who previously considered other people around them becomes increasingly self-absorbed. Fears, previously shrugged off, now become consuming. Everything in the person's life begins to swing to extremes. They become consumed with the need to fulfill the wants of the body, whether it be with sex, food, drugs, or anything else their bodies may demand. The body now controls the person rather than the person controlling the body. The mind, will, or emotions become the master rather than the servant. Confusion becomes the norm rather than the exception. Such a person becomes totally enslaved to their desires, although things may seem to be quite normal. Even if someone attempts to expose their problems they have an explanation for their behavior and, thus, are unable to receive it.

Fortunately, God will not allow us go quietly into a sin-induced sleep so that we eventually die. He is ready and able to enter into whatever state we are in and bring His declaration of freedom. Yet He waits for an act of our will. Every time we move away from His plans and purposes, He places before us an undeniable choice: life or death. He will never allow us to succeed forever apart from Him. We can never enjoy peace and completeness outside of His will for our lives. That's because God's will for our lives brings life, while our will always brings death. Once we have had enough of death and our own will, our response is always:

"Father, I want out - today I choose your life!"

CHAPTER

2

Purification: Getting Rid of Impurities

Passover Cup #1

God outlined the pattern of deliverance from evil in the story of Israel's exodus from Egypt (Exodus chapters 3-15). He has preserved the knowledge of that process throughout history in the Passover celebration. Even today, four cups of wine are raised during the Passover Seder Meal, each detailing the process by which we are saved, healed, delivered, and freed. The first Passover cup is known as Purification. It represents that work of God in our lives by which He cleanses us from all our impurities. God's work always begins here, even as this is the first cup lifted during the Passover Seder Meal.

In this chapter we will look in detail at God's work of purification in our lives. What is God's purification? How does His purification impact me today? What does purification have to do with delivering me from evil? These are some of the questions that we will seek to answer.

Before we can know a real purifying in our lives, we must be sure that we are seeking it with the right motives. The key is that we must be totally honest before God. He will give us our heart's desires as long as they match His will. Asking to be delivered from evil matches God's will, since that is how He taught us to pray in the Lord's Prayer. However, there is often a difference between what we say we want and what we really want. I may ask to be delivered, but do I really want to be delivered from evil, or am I simply tired of paying the price for sin? It is easy to show remorse for a crime after a person has been caught. We may say we want to be delivered yet there may still be a part of us that enjoys the sin.

The children of Israel might have been content if God had merely rescued them from slavery in Egypt. In fact, every Jewish person celebrating Passover today reads aloud in the Seder liturgy "Dayenu", which means "It would have been enough":

"If God had only brought us out of Egypt, but had not punished the Egyptians – Dayenu.

If God had only punished the Egyptians, but had not destroyed their gods – Dayenu.

If God had only destroyed their gods, but had not slain their firstborn – Dayenu..."

If God had removed the chains of bondage, yet left Israel in Egypt, it would have been enough. However, His plans for them were much greater than being free, yet remaining in a foreign land. God had a destiny for Israel to fulfill beyond merely removing them from trouble (though it certainly included that). If God had merely set them free, yet kept them in Egypt, they would have missed all of the wonders that occurred throughout their history, such as at Sinai and Jericho, as well as through individuals as Samson, Samuel, David, and Solomon, to name a few. God's plan involved Israel's removal from hostile territory so that they could inherit their own land. His interest in Israel was greater than freeing them from the shackles of slavery. In fact, the full ramifications of God's deliverance of Israel are yet to be seen when Messiah Himself reigns on earth!

Similarly, God has purposed to bring us into the life He has designed for us, walking in His will for our lives. This is far greater than we could ever imagine. In fact, God has told us that we cannot possibly fathom what He has in mind for us! That is a good thing. Since His plan is infinitely more than we can envision we are forced to leave the details to Him. Even if we wanted to, we couldn't plan our own deliverance and freedom. How can we plot a path, since we really don't know where we are or where we are going?

If you had asked an Israelite living at the time of Moses what their trouble in Egypt was, most Israelites would have perceived their problem to be a ruthless king and the backbreaking work he was forcing them to do. They would, of course, have been right, since these troubles were very real. This was, at least, the immediate cause of their problems. However, these problems were merely symptoms of their real problem. Their physical enslavement in Egypt was merely the result of their true problem with evil. It resulted from decisions made much earlier in their history, by which they had embraced non-God-centered desires. Left alone, these early desires would have resulted in Israel losing its own identity and taking on the culture of Egypt. However, it was slavery that prevented Israel from being assimilated into the Egyptian culture. If the nation had not become made slaves in Egypt we might not have a Jewish people today! Even so, Israel's perception of their problem (slavery in Egypt) was merely symptomatic of a greater root problem with evil.

Prior to receiving their inheritance and taking the land promised to Abraham, Israel needed to have the root of their problems dealt with. While being physically owned by Pharaoh, they were spiritually owned by the gods of Egypt. These gods had made their way into the Israelite culture and lifestyle; so much so, that Ra was as much a god to Israel as the God of Abraham was. That is why that the battle in Egypt was a fight between the Lord and the false gods of Egypt, between the true

God and fallen heavenly powers. Each of the plagues God had sent was a means of exposing the various Egyptian gods. Before the Lord, each of these gods was shown to be impotent. And each plague solidified God's sovereignty in the hearts of the Israelites, while releasing another god's hold on their affections. This was not done haphazardly, but purposely, as God exposed each of the false gods before Israel, demonstrating His sovereignty over each one.

At the time of the exodus, God had no interest in Pharaoh or the Egyptian people in terms of saving them. Their time would come later. Nor was He interested in teaching Egypt a lesson through the plagues and subsequent departure of Israel from their midst. Their time of salvation would come with the rest of the world when the work of Jesus Christ was revealed. In fact, during the exodus, God desired that Pharaoh fight against Him so that His people would not only be delivered, but also freed! God was using evil, therefore, to purify the hearts of His people. God used evil to create repulsion to evil in the hearts of Israel. By the time that God was finished with Pharaoh and Egypt, Israel would want nothing to do with them. Israel's ties with Egypt and her gods were being permanently severed.

The same thing is true in our own lives. While we are often deceived into thinking that we know what the root of our troubles is, God truly does know and often uses trouble to expose it. More often than not, the root of our troubles is much different than what we may believe. Fortunately, it doesn't matter what we may think the problems are, or if we understand the true cause of our troubles, for God knows what the true source of trouble is and He will expose it. He will deal with what is truly important. Israel perceived the slavery to be the root of all their troubles, and so their cry to God was for deliverance from slavery. God responded to Israel's true need, and in the process the perceived problem was dealt with as well. When God dealt with the spiritual problem, the physical problem melted away and they received what they really needed.

Just as Israel's flight from bondage to freedom began when they cried out to the Lord because of their pain and suffering, our freedom today begins the same way. When the pain or suffering becomes overwhelming, we cry out. We may not understand everything going on or the real source of our troubles, but we do know that it hurts and we want to be delivered. We do not have all the answers, but we know that things are not right. So, we cry out "Abba, Father!"

Both physical and emotional pain is designed by God to be a warning to us. Without pain we would never know that something is wrong. There is no motivation to cry out to God for help without pain. Yet no one likes pain. We avoid it whenever possible, looking for the nearest sources of relief.

In this day and age we have become experts in numbing pain. Today, mind and emotion numbing drugs are prescribed and administered before even a basic search for a root cause of a person's problems is instigated. It is true that drugs can be a part of the healing process. However, our use of drugs in this society borders on the ridiculous. As a result many of God's children are walking around oppressed by evil and unable to cry out to Him. For them, there is no need to cry out to God for His sovereign intervention because the pain has been masked, even though the root problem still exists.

A few years ago, I went to visit an ear specialist to see if he could get rid of a ringing I have had in my ears for the last twenty years. After a five-minute examination, the doctor informed me that the ringing was permanent and that I would have to get used to it. In the same breath he told me (in all seriousness) that if the noise in my head drove me to the point of wanting to kill myself he would write me a prescription for an anti-depressant. I walked out of that office wondering if I looked miserable enough to need drugs. Yet I couldn't believe it! I could get an anti-depressant from an ear doctor! I knew I could call him at any time and get an emotion-numbing drug because of ringing ears!

Far too often in the pastorate, I have seen people who need to cry out to the Lord for deliverance, yet who were numbed by drugs. It is almost as though an impenetrable barrier had been placed around them - a barrier that prevents anything of God from breaking through to them. Realizing our desperate situation and crying out to God is the real beginning of our deliverance. Unfortunately, drugs can often complicate the process. Yet when people are in pain and do cry out to Him,

God responds by initiating a process that results in the sons of God being revealed in power (Romans 8). The process is designed not only to meet the immediate needs of the individual or group in trouble, but also to further the kingdom of God on planet Earth. It is a process beginning with purification and the exposing and dethroning of evil. It ends with the glory of God being revealed through His people. It starts in oppression and ends in authority.

I once knew a woman who was plagued with deep problems. Some days she would lie catatonic on the bed all day, while other days she would be in a fog. She was never happy and had difficulty interacting with people. If life didn't go as she planned everyone around her paid a price. As a result she had few friends. She jumped from psychologist to pastor trying to find relief for her suffering. They treated her for depression and attempted to bolster her self-esteem by having her stand in front of a mirror and tell herself what a good person she was. She was taught to blame the people around her for her troubles. Yet, nothing seemed to help. She became good at making others as miserable as she was. Getting married didn't help; in fact, it made things worse.

The situation grew worse when she gave birth to a son and buried her mother within a three-month span. Life, while difficult to live before, was now impossible to endure. Demonic dreams, relational problems, and other things came marching in. For six straight months she got a first hand look at the evil that had controlled her life. At the end of that period she was at the end of her rope. Totally desperate, she was ready for any solution. She knew that things had to change. Yet she wondered if a solution to her problems was even available. Then someone suggested that God could remove the source of the pain. She was a little skeptical but concluded that if God could help her she would jump at the opportunity.

Just a few days later she sat face to face with an older woman who told her entire life story back to her. The older woman exposed the true evil in the younger woman's life: rejection. Within a matter of hours the pain built up over the years was gushing out of her body. She wailed until her small frame could take no more. Soon after, the demonic presence in her life was manifested and dealt with. Within minutes the

Lord Jesus touched the woman with His acceptance and love. She saw Him! She felt Him! She was instantly changed! In fact, she has never been the same! The evil in her life was exposed and she was completely repulsed by it. That repulsion led to desperation for God to move on her behalf. It took six months to place the evil in her life into proper perspective. As soon as the evil became repulsive to her deliverance occurred. As soon as purification had run its course she was freed. As soon as she could cry out with an honest heart, God met her.

Trouble needs to be exposed for what it truly is. The root of the evil needs to be exposed and shown in its true form: ugly and impotent! Preparing a person for deliverance is what PURIFICATION is all about. Deliverance from evil is the easy part. When deliverance occurs it is instantaneous. Purification is the time consuming aspect of God's process to freedom. The purpose of purification is to place a true desire to be tied to God's heart and will in our own hearts. Once purification occurs, we can honestly say to God from our heart, "Deliver us from evil." When purification is finished evil is not only unwanted, it is hated. We wonder how we could have been so duped for so long by a second rate power. Once God purifies us, staying in Egypt is not an option; we have to leave! We begin to set our sights on what is yet to be.

God begins to bring people into freedom as soon as they call out to Him. We, as Christians, have an incredible opportunity to join God as He works. Whether praying for God to change a life, speaking truth into that life, or witnessing God deliver one of His own, we enjoy the wonder of heavenly intervention in the affairs of man. This intervention exposes the reality of evil in a life and initiates a journey to freedom. Exposing evil and expressing the reality of God's glory and sovereignty is what purification is all about. When purification has worked in the hearts of people deliverance cannot be stopped. When the dam begins to crack, watch out! The rushing waters of deliverance will tear down the walls. When purification has run its course, deliverance has to follow! Freedom has to come! Freedom will come!

Shaping the Will

God wants to deliver us and bring us freedom. He wants us to be living to our fullest potential. Christ Himself came that we might have life abundant, both full and free. Yet God will never violate our will. If we don't want deliverance, He will honor our wishes. If we don't want to leave Egypt, He will never send Moses. The choice to obey is always in our hands.

Yet our human nature often works against us. Even if I want to be delivered from evil, a part of me still enjoys sin. There is a war between my flesh and spirit, between the newly saved man and my old nature. This fact raises a problem. As long as a part of me is enjoying sin, I will be unable to cry out honestly to God for deliverance. Yet God is well aware of our dilemma and takes the first step. He begins a process that shapes our desires, placing them in line with His own. As soon as we cry out for help God starts the process of purification to change our desires. He will respond to any cry to remove the results of sin by shaping our heart so that we cry out for what we really need. God uses purification to bring us to the place where we really want to be delivered. He takes our desire to be freed from the penalty for sin and loosed from slavery and builds on it, changing us enough so that we ask Him to give us His mind.

When I was growing up a common punishment for a boy caught smoking was to force him to smoke the entire cigar in the presence of his father. What was cool in the mind of the young boy became embarrassing as the cigar smell permeated everything. The first few puffs were often handled well, yet few boys endured to the end without turning green and getting ill. The act of smoking that had seemed a grown up thing to do was now associated with the vile. What had been cool was now repulsive.

God's process of handling our sin and the evil it produces is very similar. He allows us to see the evil first hand and glimpse the true nature of what we are involved with. God also keeps that evil in front of us until we are sick of it. He gives us enough of a look at evil to see the true cost of being dominated by it.

Like any father, God wisely allows the evil in our lives to be revealed. The true nature and purpose of evil is exposed to those who are controlled by it. The individual can look and see the horror of what has held them captive. The heart is changed as the attitude regarding the sin changes. When we see the true nature of the thing that has held us captive we want to be freed from it. We want God to take that evil out of our lives. Yet seeing evil is never fun. Having evil placed in front of us is not our idea of a good time, but God is faithful and will give us every opportunity to make the right choices in our life. The choices He places before us are never difficult: life or death, prosperity or destruction, sickness or health, etc.... The decision is never hard. Even the most self-centered will make the right choice. How God brings us to make these choices is another matter.

The prophet Hosea gives us a picture of just how God accomplishes this. By giving us this picture God reveals how He will respond to our own rebellion. This is helpful in teaching us how to pray for someone who is traveling a path they should not be. In addition, we can understand how God will deal with us if we try to walk away from Him. Hosea was commanded to marry a prostitute named Gomer, a woman who was living a life of total rebellion. She did not understand the ways of God, nor had she any idea how God designed her to live. Gomer was a poster child for a self-centered life. She did not have the ability to function within a normal marriage relationship. Still Hosea married her. Their marriage then became a visible sign to Israel of their own relationship to God.

God had tied Himself by covenant to Israel. Yet many in Israel lived a life of rebellion during the time of Hosea. They did not understand the ways of God and, therefore, had no idea how God had designed them to live. They did not have the ability to function within a covenant relationship. That being the case, God revealed His plan to bring them back to Himself. Hosea 2:6-7 says,

> "Therefore, behold, I will hedge up thy way with thorns, and make a wall, that she shall not find her paths. And she shall

> *follow after her lovers, but she shall not overtake them; and she shall seek them, but shall not find them: then shall she say, I will go and return to my first husband; for then was it better with me than now."*

God would not allow Israel to prosper. In fact, He was going to make life unbearable for her. She would try to travel down her own path, but not be able to find her way. She would attempt to live her life, but the normal way of life would not work anymore. What worked in the past would now be frustrated. Life would become a chore. While her lover should have been the Lord God, she continually chased after other lovers, though she could never catch them. She tried to be satisfied by things other than the Lord, yet there was no satisfaction. What was easy to enjoy before was now impossible to find.

When God purifies, we can't live the way we lived before. He takes the things that satisfied us before and puts them out of reach. He totally frustrates what we previously took for granted. Sin loses its glamour so that we can no longer enjoy it. Simply finding a way to enjoy sin becomes difficult. This is what God did to Israel while they were enslaved in Egypt. Life became unbearable for them. The same was true of Israel in the time of Hosea. This picture is repeated countless times in Scripture. It is no different today. When we embrace sin and live in rebellion, God makes life unbearable for us. Purification is painful and usually takes a long time, because we, typically, are very stubborn. Too often we hold on to the things God wants removed from our lives until the bitter end.

The fires of purification are intense. Sometimes we may try to short-circuit the process. However, God will not allow our life to change until our heart and our attitude towards sin has changed. This is how the Apostle John could say in 3 John 1:2,

> "Beloved, I wish above all things that thou mayest prosper and be in health, even as thy soul prospereth."

CHAPTER 2

The Apostle John understood that true prosperity was tied to the condition of a person's heart. If the heart was beating apart from the heart of God, prosperity would not be found. On the other hand, if the heart beats according to the heart of God, prosperity and health will follow. Enjoying success, happiness, and contentment in life is directly related to being in God's plan for our lives. Purification changes our heart (which is wicked above all else) into a warm heart tied to God's own heart.

As quickly as purification has run its course, God changes the entire atmosphere of life. Hosea 2:14 gives us a look at the change.

> *"Therefore, behold, I will allure her, and bring her into the wilderness, and speak comfortably unto her."*

Once we turn back to the Lord, He moves us to a place where we are alone with Him. We are then at the place where the influence of sin cannot touch us. In fact, we couldn't sin if we wanted to. There are no enemies to fight. We are hidden in a secluded place, ready to enter into a new relationship with a loving, jealous God.

Understanding how purification works gives us added weapons to use when praying for people who are living outside of God's plan. When we know that God does not want a person to live outside of His plan for them, we can easily pray according to God's will. The same is true when we know that God does not want them to prosper in life apart from Him. When we see someone living in sin we can begin to pray that God will frustrate the plans of Satan in his or her life and straighten all the crooked paths. We can begin to pray that God will make life unbearable apart from Him and that the longing of their heart will be for the Lord Himself. We can begin to pray prayers like, "Lord, make finding their way to sin difficult." "Father, make them tired of trying to find their lovers... make sin painful to them." "Father, turn their attention upward." "Lord, let them see the wonder of who you are and be drawn to you." These types of prayers change lives and send people running to God. They take impossible, hopeless situations and turn them around. These prayers take people who are left for dead, and turn them into vibrant examples of the love, mercy and glory of God.

God is faithful. He who has invited us to fulfill a destiny which He ordained before He said, "Let there be light," is faithful to purify us completely. The Lord is faithful to make life in sin unbearable for us. He will frustrate our plans so that we run to Him and change our heart, so that we can cry out to Him, "Deliver us from evil."

Being In Purification

Understanding what life is like while we are being purified is important because purification and redemption can look the same. However, the major difference between the two is our relationship to God in each. By asking the question, "Where is God in the process?" we can begin to understand the difference between them.

The life of a person living in sin is summed up by one word: oppression. As evil is running its course in a person's life, their days are full of troubles. They commonly feel frustrated and, at times, the weight may seem unbearable. Life just isn't right, and problems seem to build on each other. New problems appear just as life seems to be looking better.

When someone is living under the weight of sin they have a difficult time understanding freedom. Even though they may desire to change, understanding what a life of freedom is remains beyond their comprehension. When they are told that God is going to free them, the response is often guarded and unsure.

This was certainly the case when the children of Israel lived in oppression in Egypt. Trouble and frustration were a normal part of their lives. They cried out to the Lord and, hearing them, He sent Moses with a message of freedom. Yet Israel could not understand the full implication of Moses' message from God. They responded to Moses while still yoked to the evil that controlled them. As the process of purification unfolded and the plagues were released, the normal life of an Israelite in Egypt changed dramatically. God's actions through Moses towards Pharaoh rocked the boat. "Didn't Moses know that Pharaoh could kill them?" "Didn't Moses know that challenging the Egyptians was not very smart?" Many of the Israelites in Egypt were overwhelmed with fear as God began His work to sanctify them. Scared and uncertain of their future, the only thing they knew for sure was that life was about to change dramatically whether they liked it or not.

While the plagues were being released there was no glorious cloud or pillar of fire. The manifest presence of God was not holding their hands, nor did they see the wonders of His face calming them as He worked. What Israel saw was their normal lives being systematically dismantled before them. Their home, where they had lived for the past four hundred years, was being taken out from under them. They saw the opportunity for their destruction rather than their salvation.

It is no different with us. When God sanctifies, He forces our hearts to bow before Him. False gods are dethroned, as He becomes the sole Ruler in our lives. This is scary at first, and may seem to be for our destruction rather than our freedom. Our lives as we have known them begin to unravel. Yet God is faithful to purify His people. He will move His hand to cause our hearts to bow before Him and bring us into His life. Feeling God's hand in our life is much different than seeing His face. In the church we love to see the Lord's face and get a glimpse of His glory. This is wondrous and always results in seeing God move on our behalf as His grace is given to us. When we see His face all is well in the world. His favor permeates our lives.

Yet having the Lord's hand on us is difficult. When God places His hand on us, most often it is on the back of our necks! In purification, we have the hand of the Lord on us. He takes our heads and plants them in the ground. He brings His sovereignty into our lives. He is causing our hearts to bow before Him.

We can't see God when His hand is on us. We know that He is there because we feel the pressure of His hand pushing our heads down. But seeing His face is impossible. God is bowing our heads before Him so that the oppression will slide right off our shoulders. Oppression can't stay on the shoulder bowed before God's throne. Yet because we can't see Him we can easily feel like we are on the outside of the church looking in. We can't seem to fit in with the rest of the body. Other people may seem to have it all together, while we are a major basket case. Still, God is at work. He will bow our hearts before Him and we will be free. Take heart! The time of having His hand on us will end and we will see His face. We will take our place within the body of Christ and we will no longer be an outcast. All we must to do is endure, holding on until God has finished the work at hand.

Enduring tribulation is a major theme of the New Testament. We are admonished to trust that God will sanctify us. We are told that tribulation (or pressure) brings nothing but good in our lives. Tribulation breeds endurance. Endurance brings a changed heart that is approved by God. This change of character births hope. We begin to expect the fulfillment of God's word. We begin to live knowing that we will see the reality of God in our lives. We begin to live knowing that our life will change! The End Will Come and We Will Live!

Endurance is based in trust. A person who trusts God says, "It does not matter what I see nor how I feel. This pressure may kill me, but I place myself in the hands of God who is Lord of all! If this pleases You, Lord, then it pleases me! Though He slay me, yet will I trust in Him!

Lord;
I trust You! Do with me as You wish! I confess that I have sinned. I am living separated from You. What I have entertained is wrong! I need You to intervene in my life. Change me God!

CHAPTER

3

The Night of Deliverance

God's process to bring His people from bondage to freedom includes four steps: Purification, Deliverance, Redemption, and Praise. There are few requirements as we are being brought through this process. In fact, once the process has begun very few actions can stop it. God does all the work by placing people in a position where their feelings and reactions naturally fit His plan for their deliverance. God molds the mind, will, and emotions to act and desire in line with what He has planned. Realistically, it is difficult (if not impossible) for a person being delivered to do anything wrong. Their path is ordained and controlled by God who knows the condition of the heart and is changing it for His purpose.

The responsibilities of those being freed are limited and easily accomplished. As a general principle, we do not have a list to follow, therefore, there is no way that we can slow it down through our own actions. Nor can we speed it up. It is God who changes the heart. If He was merely changing the mind, we might be able to have some say in the matter, since the mind is something within our control. However the heart is another matter. This principle is true throughout the process with the single exception: of the "Night of Deliverance." That night is absolutely unique.

On that night a battle erupts in the spiritual realm - a battle that will invade the physical realm. The devastation will affect anything and everyone in the land who is not protected by God. God is about to unleash the final plague on the gods of Egypt, and He does not want His people to be a part of it. God does not need man's help that evening. He has prepared all parties for the coming events beginning with Moses at the burning bush. The stage is set and the first steps of His personal interaction with His people are about to be seen. He is about to show His almighty hand by physically intervening in the lives of His people. Tonight the relationship between God and His people is going to take a giant leap forward. Life will become instantaneously different for every person claimed by God.

That night is a night of choice. Men and women will either demonstrate that they are tied to God and a part of Israel, or else pay the price along with Egypt and its gods. That night every one must decide whether they are in or out. Yet the choice is not that difficult. Israel had already seen the defeat of the gods of Egypt and knew that God was sovereign. Their choice, therefore, was between slavery and freedom, death or life, Pharaoh or God. It really was not a difficult choice to make because God had worn out their welcome in the land of slavery. Soon they will no longer be welcome in Egypt. So people must decide that evening to either leave Egypt with Israel, or be an outcast.

It is no different with us. At the heart of our relationship with God is our free will. We have the choice of masters to serve; either to choose God as our sovereign or choose Pharaoh. We have a choice as to whether or not we will love the Lord and embrace His will for our lives. When God delivers His own children, the deliverance comes by their own free will. We desire to be delivered and tied to God. That is what purification is all about—it brings us to the point where we must have God. Our lives must be engulfed in His life or we will die. The Night of Deliverance puts us to the test. It demonstrates to all our readiness for freedom.

Chapter 3

Deliverance was never designed by God to be a spectator sport. When we think of deliverance, it often conjures up images of a Christian standing over a catatonic individual who remains unconscious until an exorcism is accomplished. Someone observing it would think that the focus of deliverance was the interaction between a saint and the demonic. However God designed a process that involves the person being delivered as well. After all, they are the ones being delivered from evil and freed to God. Deliverance is between them and God. Deliverance is about a person being freed to wonder in amazement at their living, liberating God. The person being delivered is expected to acknowledge the acts of God and make a stand, agreeing with Him. The heart of the person is the key to all the actions and activities surrounding their freedom. The Night of Deliverance, therefore, is a sort of graduation party. The events of the Night of Deliverance declares to all that God has been given the sovereign right to rule and protect a life! The Night of Deliverance tells all that Purification has run its course. Evil has been made odious and the person is ready and waiting for freedom.

Purification takes the initial desire for freedom and makes the heart desire it all the more. Purification makes the heart cry out to God, "Deliver us from evil." On the Night of Deliverance, the heart is put to the test. The prepared heart now has an opportunity to prove itself. On the Night of Deliverance four requirements are placed before the people; four simple (yet bold) tasks are set before the people that will permanently separate them unto Him. Meeting the four requirements demonstrates that the heart is ready for God's deliverance and bowed before His sovereignty. When the four requirements are met a person is declaring that they have had enough of Egypt and are ready to trust God. These four requirements include:

1. **Applying the Blood to the Doorpost**
2. **Eating the Lamb and Unleavened Bread**
3. **Staying in the House**
4. **Being Ready to Leave**

These tasks given to Israel were not overwhelming. They did not require great concentration or forethought. Yet their deliverance was contingent on following these instructions. It is no different today. If we are going to be delivered we must walk through these steps as well. Even the person who needs deliverance from demonic forces must go through them. The reason is simple: God wants the person being freed to demonstrate their desire to be tied to Him. When the person being delivered walks through these steps evil has no chance. No force in heaven or on earth will prevent deliverance and freedom coming to one of His own who applies these four steps.

Deliverance always comes to the heart that honestly asks God for help. Helping someone walk through the four requirements of the Passover night will permanently rebuke evil from a life every time. When the tormented person applies the blood, eats the Passover Lamb and Unleavened Bread, stays in the house, and gets ready to leave freedom is insured. It will be a lasting freedom that will never know bondage again!

God's process to freedom (purification, deliverance, redemption, praise) and the instructions given to Israel just prior to their deliverance (apply the blood, eat the lamb, stay in the house, be ready to leave) are all elements of the Passover. For thousands of years the Jewish people have celebrated God's pathway to freedom. In addition, each of the Passover elements we have discussed was fulfilled by Christ. What God is asking of us therefore is nothing new. Christ has already prepared us for it. All that we need to do is walk in what Jesus has already accomplished. Once our heart truly longs for God, all that we need to do is apply to our own lives the finished work of our Savior. The physical actions that Israel carried out that first Passover night can be applied spiritually in our lives today. We can walk through the elements of that first Passover night and claim the victory of the cross and empty tomb, as well as witness the sovereign Lord remove the curse of evil from our lives.

If God has you in the process of purification, you can personally walk through these short steps. When evil has been exposed in your life, so that sin now looks odious to you, walk through these four truths and deliverance and freedom will come. If the task seems overwhelming to you, ask a brother or sister in the Lord to walk with you. God wants you to be protected, delivered, and free of all evil. God wants you to be freed to Him! When you are at the end of yourself and desperate for God, apply the blood, eat the lamb, stay in the house, and be ready to leave. Your God will meet you in the land of your sin and bring you out. He will meet you where you are, to deliver you from evil.

Applying the Blood to the Doorpost

From the beginning of human history, God made it clear that there was something special about blood. When Cain killed Abel, God heard the blood of Abel crying out to Him from the ground. Later, when Noah was given a covenant, God specifically singled out the blood. Noah was told not to spill the blood (kill) or drink blood from any source. In giving these instructions, God was declaring that blood was significant to Him. He was demonstrating that there was something special about the blood. These commands have permeated every society and culture since the flood. Every person alive has an inner knowing that blood is to be respected and not misused. Every person knows that spilling the blood of a person or the drinking of blood is repulsive and to be disdained. Those people who do misuse blood are most often considered outcasts of society or cultists. It is for this reason we lock up murderers. We limit our contact with those who are found to drink any type of blood. If nothing else, we relegate such people to the ranks of the insane.

The significance of blood became even clearer as the Torah was given to Israel. Leviticus 17:11 states that life itself is found in the blood. The life of all flesh whether man or animal is found in the blood. The ramifications for us are enormous and cover many areas of life. For example it settles forever the debate over when life begins. If there is blood, there is life. It is that simple.

A myriad of sacrifices also declared the place of blood before God. Blood was so significant before God that there was no atonement for sin apart from the blood. The shedding of blood was required for sins to be forgiven. Blood had to be presented before a restoration of relationship with God could take place. One sacrifice after another declared a specific path to forgiveness through the presentation of blood.

The repulsion to the misuse of blood was deeply engrained in Jewish teachings. A heavy penalty was exacted from a killer or a person who misused blood in any way. This repulsion to the misuse of blood was so engrained in the Jewish thought of Christ's day that it eventually cost the Lord most of His disciples (see John 6). On that day, He told His disciples (which numbered around seventy at the time) that they could have no part of Him unless they ate His body and drank His blood. Before the end of the day, the number of disciples was drastically reduced to twelve. Imagine losing eighty-three percent of your congregation from one message. Those who walked away from the Lord that day had good reason to leave. What those defecting disciples heard stood in direct opposition to the Scriptures. If they had only been willing to stick around they would have understood the depths of what Christ was really saying.

All of God's commands regarding blood were brought into perspective when the Lord Jesus walked the earth. All of the sacrifices outlined in the Torah were perfectly fulfilled. All of God's requirements for the shedding of blood were satisfied by the work of Jesus Christ. While the Lord was still on earth, He drew special attention to one of these sacrifices in particular: the Passover sacrifice. When the Lord explained this sacrifice to His disciples He finally brought understanding to the twelve men who remained with Him when so many others left.

On the night that the Lord was betrayed He held His final Passover Seder on earth. During the meal, the Lord lifted up a cup of wine and declared, "This is My blood of a new covenant, which is shed for many for the remission of sins." What an amazing statement! The blood of the Son of God, the spotless Lamb of God was to be shed so that many could have a restored relationship with the Father. As a result, anyone who would accept the blood covering of Jesus Christ would be restored to a proper standing with heaven.

Today, when a person accepts Jesus Christ as their Savior and Lord they come under the blood sacrifice of the Lamb of God. We take the blood and life of the Lord into ourselves. Because of the blood sacrifice the relationship with heaven lost in the Garden of Eden is restored. God forgives sin and restores us to our proper place within His Kingdom. God places each person brought under His authority by the blood covenant in a specific place, which He designed from the beginning of time. The blood of Jesus becomes the sign of a significant relationship between the throne of God and a person, or group of people. The blood places us into the incredible category of being citizens of heaven, children of the living God. It is the Blood of Jesus Christ that gives us our identity by providing atonement for our sins and our previous separation from God. The blood of Jesus Christ the Messiah corrects the wrongs and sets things back to right.

Every year our Messianic Jewish brothers and sisters celebrate the Passover along with the rest of the Jewish community worldwide. When the Messianic Jew raises the Cup of Redemption, they see the restoring work of the Messiah. They celebrate the restoration of the tie between heaven and earth as they remember God's redemption of the Israelites in Egypt. Whenever communion is served throughout the church we see the restoring work of Jesus the Christ. We celebrate the union of God with man through Jesus Christ. The blood of our Lord has a special place in our hearts and lives.

Yet we are not the only ones who see the blood of Jesus as significant. Every spiritual being in heaven and on earth must respect the blood of Jesus. When the blood of Jesus is seen applied to a life, all creatures in heaven and earth know that the person has come under the authority and reign of Jesus Christ. They know that the person belongs to, and is protected by the authority of God Himself. Every spiritual being understands that if they touch the life before them, they are touching God. Every power, principality and demon knows that the life covered by the blood of the Lamb is under the control of His Majesty.

How, then do we apply the blood of Jesus as we are waiting for our deliverance? We begin by recalling that the blood of the Passover Lamb was applied to the doorpost. The blood of the lamb became a visible sign that the family living in the house was Israelite and, therefore, belonged to God. They did not belong in the Egyptian culture. In the same way today, applying the blood of Jesus is also a visible sign. We apply the Blood of the Lamb by declaring to all around us, visible and invisible, that we under the authority of heaven itself and are, therefore, owned by God! We do not belong to the society in which we are bound. We no longer belong to this slave culture. Yet making this declaration is an act of faith. If we believe that God has the authority in our lives, and that His word will be accomplished, we must act accordingly.

The result of believing His word is that we are satisfied and never thirst again. The blood of the Lamb is taken within our lives and applied for all to see. Our act of believing the Messiah is the spiritual act of drinking His blood. When we say, "Yes Lord, You are right and true", we are taking Him within ourselves. When we declare that belief to all around us, we apply the blood of the Lamb to our lives. It sounds out a clear note to all that will hear that we stand in line with the declarations of heaven. We declare that we agree with what God has said, so that His thoughts are our thoughts, His mind our mind. He is in us and we are in Him!

We also declare to the evil, the simple message that it no longer has any dominion in our lives. I am now declaring that I have come under the authority of God and am separated to God. I am made holy. That means that Christ Jesus has placed the sign of ownership on me. Any issues of ownership, therefore, must be addressed to Him. So must any attempts to influence my life. Look at His Blood. All must respect His right of ownership.

We apply the Blood of Christ as an outward sign. All powers and principalities must respect the authority of Jesus in the life that He has claimed. The forces of evil do not respect people. Nor do they fear man. Evil will not run from a human being. Evil will, however, and must bow to the authority and power of Jesus Christ. The powers of darkness know that all authority in heaven and on earth has been given to Him. They know that He is the Son of God, with all the rights and privileges that go along with the position. When a life is placed under the authority of Christ, all must respect the Lord's right of ownership. Nothing can be done to or with a person belonging to the Kingdom of heaven without the expressed permission of either the person or the Lord Himself. Declaring ourselves to be under the Blood of Jesus, we announce that all decisions regarding our life have been deferred to the King Himself. "If you want to mess with me, you have to get past my Lord first!"

When we apply the Blood of Christ, the blood alone is what the powers of evil will see. They can't see past the blood to gaze at us. All evil can see is the authority of Christ. Evil must submit to the plans and purposes of heaven. When the Blood of Christ is seen, the free reign of terror in a life has just stopped. Evil cannot pursue that life anymore. Now all activity must be approved by heaven first - and heaven will not allow evil to do anything that does not benefit the child of God and the plans of God. The evil that previously ruled now becomes the servant.

These facts are freeing to us. As we declare our heavenly ownership, what we were and what we have done doesn't matter anymore. That's because it's not about me but all about Him! It's not about how good or bad I may look. It's about Him and what He has chosen to do. It doesn't matter how I feel or what my life may be like. He has made the rules. He is in charge. It doesn't matter what anyone may say. God has spoken His word and that word will be fulfilled in my life.

Eating the Passover Lamb and the Unleavened Bread

Eating the Passover Lamb and the Unleavened Bread was done within the house. God was establishing a protected zone for each family to stay within so that the authority of God would protect each house. The people still lived in a hostile land. Their welcome in Egypt, their home for the past four hundred years, was soon wearing out. Yet within the confines of their houses a very intimate and special event was occurring.

The Israelites were commanded to eat the Passover Lamb. The lamb had been selected out of the flock and had been living almost as a pet with the family so that it became very dear to the family before being eaten. The lamb was to be killed in a specific manner, as well as the preparations to eat it. The Unleavened Bread also had to be prepared and eaten in a ritualistic manner. Both the preparation and consumption of the Passover Lamb and the Unleavened Bread had been designed by God to be engrained in the minds of His people. What they were doing was significant even if they didn't understand it at the time. The Israelites were never to forget their time in Egypt, God's deliverance, and the freedom they were soon to enjoy. This information was to be passed down to all generations so that Israel would remember the Passover forever.

No Israelite alive at the time of the Exodus from Egypt could have imagined the true significance of what they were celebrating. In fact, they probably did not realize they were involved in a celebration at all. They were merely doing as they had been instructed, knowing that change was in the wind. They could not have comprehended that the Passover Lamb and the Unleavened Bread were both symbols of the very Son of God Himself, nor that God was outlining His plan for their freedom for all generations to follow. This plan of freedom applied not only to individual lives, but the redemption of the world in the future as well! The symbolism of the Passover Lamb and the Unleavened Bread shined like a beacon through the centuries to the time of Christ.

Even though most in Israel did not recognize Him at the time that He appeared, Jesus was the fulfillment of the Passover sacrifice. Messiah was also the fulfillment of the Unleavened Bread. While on earth the Lord commanded that all in relationship with God were now to eat Him. Jesus revealed that He was the Passover Lamb, and just as the Passover lamb was eaten after slain, so He Himself must be eaten. But how was the Lord to be eaten? And why?

To answer that question it is important to remember that God was not interested in merely giving human beings access to His Kingdom. He really wanted the restoration of the intimate relationship He had with Adam and Eve in the Garden of Eden. God wanted mankind to live and rule and relate as He had established at the beginning. The goal was that mankind might be tied into His very nature and being.

And since God Himself is one made up of three persons (Father, Son, and Holy Spirit), it was His purpose that men and women join that unity, and intimately experience being joined to His being. In John 14:20, Jesus put it this way,

"I am in the Father, and ye in me, and I in you."

The symbolism of the Passover elements pointed to an intimate relationship with the Creator, a spiritual joining where two walk as one. This intimacy was designed to be so intense that an onlooker would not be able to tell where one being stopped and the other started. When an onlooker saw a person who had taken Christ into himself or herself, the onlooker would see Jesus. By looking at a human being they would see God and catch a glimpse of heaven itself!

Understanding and walking in an intimate relationship with God was so important to God that He gave us multiple pictures of this oneness in our lives. One of the clearest can be seen in the marriage relationship: a man and a woman living together as two separate entities, yet becoming one whole being. He no longer views a husband and wife as two separate people, but as one entity. That this oneness achieved in marriage is important can be seen in what God says regarding divorce. If you doubt this truth and you are married, try praying when you are having marital problems; it is impossible. For those who are married, seeing God's blessings and success in life will be dependent on the oneness lived between husband, wife, and heaven.

Another picture of oneness that God gave us is that of the Body of Christ itself: Many parts making a complete being. As with marriage, the blessings and success enjoyed by the Body of Christ will be dependent on our oneness with each other and heaven. Taking Christ within ourselves is the only way to walk in this oneness. Oneness within the Body of Christ can only occur as a result of the restoration of our relationship with God. Our ability to live as one depends on "Christ in us, the hope of glory", and the degree to which we are willing to release His Spirit working through us!

Eating the body of the Lord Jesus was so important to the Father, that God established it as a precedent fifteen hundred years before Christ took His first step on earth. Beginning in the land of Egypt, God's people ate the Passover Lamb and the Unleavened Bread as a dress rehearsal for the coming Messiah. Today, this symbolism is still carried out within the Passover and Communion celebrations. These physical reminders of a spiritual reality are still with us today. Furthermore, inasmuch as God has placed such importance on this event, the fulfillment of the symbolism is clear. Again, Jesus said in John 6:35,

> *"I am the bread of life: he that cometh to Me shall never hunger; and he that believeth in Me shall never thirst."*

The way we eat the Passover Lamb and Unleavened Bread is to go to Jesus and stay in His presence! We must live where He is! We come to Him and never leave! We live our lives as Mary, the sister of Martha and Lazarus, did by sitting at His feet. Wherever He goes, we go. When He stops, we stop. We say with Moses, "If you do not go with us, we will not go!" It is in His presence that our need for food is satisfied. It is in His presence that we absorb the Bread of Life. In His presence we find life itself. In His presence we find joy as well, which for an oppressed slave is a welcome change!

The Passover Seder and the elements of the meal that the Lord highlighted, take on special meaning to us. The sacrament of Communion takes on an excitement as we see the depths of its fulfillment. In Communion and the Passover Seder, we see the celebration of our salvation, deliverance, and freedom. We take the life of the Lord into ourselves by believing. We apply His authority to our lives by declaring that belief. We take our sustenance from the Lord by coming to Him and allowing Him to be our all in all. We stay in His presence and allow Him to rule our lives. Every time we celebrate the Passover or the Communion we are celebrating our restored relationship with God and our freedom from evil.

For those of us being saved, the Communion can become an act of faith. Just as Israel, in Egypt, declared their belonging to God prior to deliverance, we too can celebrate the Communion, and by faith declare what is soon to be. We declare to ourselves and to those around us, as well as to all powers that God's freedom is coming! We personally announce that evil will be destroyed in or lives, just as it has been for all of God's people who have come before us. We celebrate the greatness of our Messiah by believing His word, declaring it and coming to Him. Every time we lift the cup or eat the unleavened bread we remind all of our intimate relationship with our God! When we lift the cup we say, "I believe You." When we lift the bread, we say, "I come to You." The bread we take and eat becomes a visual reminder to all peoples and powers of our intimate relationship with the King of kings. He is in us and we are in Him!

As we prepare for deliverance, evil is being made odious to us. We declare to all around, God's ownership and authority in our lives. We stay connected to our Deliverer. What is the next instruction? It is to "stay in the house."

Staying In The House

Outside the walls of the house sinister events are about to occur. Within the house a sanctuary has been prepared, a safe haven to protect the family from the holocaust about to be unleashed in the land. Deliverance is eminent. Evil is about to be rebuked. The stranglehold on God's people is about to be broken.

God Himself is hovering over the house marked by the blood of the Lamb. God will not allow any harm to come to those inside. Outside the sanctuary total carnage is about to unfold. A battle is about to take place between the gods of Egypt and the hosts of the Sovereign God. A battle will unfold that will invade the physical realm with death. All of those people who are not protected by God are about to suffer loss. They will all lose someone dear to them. Those who had oppressed and extracted a price from God's people will now pay. Those who profited from the suffering of God's people will pay with that which is dearest to them: life.

God wanted His people protected during the events of the final plague. He didn't want any of His people involved in the carnage. Nor did He want them to see the carnage. The Israelites were to stay in the sanctuary. They were to be having an intimate time with God while He battled on their behalf. They were to be eating the Passover while the carnage was going on. While Israel was fulfilling the Passover commands, safely tucked away in their houses, their future was being established at the same time that their past was being cut off.

God is so amazing. He often will bring us to the point of deliverance even though we may not have a clue as to what we are being delivered from. Have you ever been worshiping the Lord and found yourself crying for no apparent reason? After the crying has stopped you feel lighter and a little freer. God has just brought freedom into your life and you may not even know how or why. God is so gentle with His children, so compassionate, so caring.

God isn't interested in our involvement with the process when we are about to be delivered. He wants us to stay in the house. God wants us to stay in the sanctuary that He has created for us so that we might have an intimate encounter with Him. While the screams may be heard from outside, the memory created within the sanctuary is one of a supernatural time with an awesome God. What survived from the night of the last plague was the Passover celebration. Although death occurred that night, what was remembered was the greatness of God. A night of death and destruction is remembered today as a celebration. In fact, part of the Passover Seder today recalls the plagues placed on the Egyptians with compassion for the Egyptian people. The true Passover celebration's focus is the restoration of a relationship with God. The focus of the celebration is not the rebuking of Egypt, but of God reclaiming His people. When true deliverance occurs the predominate memory left to the person delivered is of the Lord and not the evil rebuked.

I will never forget one woman's deliverance whose testimony has driven this point home for me and remains with me today. She was delivered from a demon in a very dramatic way with superhuman strength and a male voice coming from her. The battle with the demonic was intense. Yet, when the demonic presence was gone she saw the cross of Jesus and collapsed on the floor in a heap. She could not move a muscle in her body. When the Lord joined her, all the fear left her. The sin and evil in her life was easily left at the foot of the cross. Then He physically touched her with His love. I am not sure exactly how it happened, but we knew that it did because you could see the love of the Lord on her. Shortly after this, she regained enough strength to sit up, and, looking at me, said, "He loves me! He loves me!" as she pounded her heart with her fist. I knew immediately that her struggle was over, and that the demonic presence could never touch her again. She was totally changed. Twelve years have passed and she has never been the same. She is still telling people of a God that loves her and loves them as well! The heart had been prepared, deliverance took place, and evil was permanently rebuked.

If you were to ask her today what she remembers most about that night, she would not tell you a dramatic story of mystical and powerful demonic forces. Nor would she tell you about the superhuman strength she possessed. Rather, she would tell you of an intimate time she had with her God! She would tell you about Jesus and her awesome God, who joined her in her distress and saved her. She would tell you of a God who really loves her. She was set free, not so much from something, as she was freed to Someone! She was brought into a restored relationship with God who changed her entire way of living!

As God is preparing you for deliverance, He will build you a sanctuary and call you to an intimate time with Him. When the sanctuary is established, stay in the house. Learn to fall in love with your God while He wars on your behalf. Allow God the right to establish a place for the two of you and allow Him to take control over any power that threatens the relationship He is building with you. Stay in the house and let Him set you free.

Being Ready to Leave

When deliverance comes, it will be instantaneous. Just as a boulder, when it has been pushed off a mountain peak, will run downhill until it reaches the bottom, God's plans are in motion and they will be fulfilled. There will be no turning back. God's final instruction to those about to be delivered was "Be ready to leave; you are not staying here". How exciting! You are leaving for a place promised beforehand, a land of your own to fit in and be productive. You will be living with your own people as rulers rather than slaves. No more demands to produce for a tyrant. No more heaviness or exhaustion. No more restless nights, wondering what the future will hold. No more lack, or hunger, or pain. You will soon be on your way.

How does God want you to prepare for the journey ahead? Pack light and be ready to leave at a moment's notice. You will not know the exact time He will declare your liberty, but when He does you will be moving out immediately. You may sense that the time is near, yet only God knows the time of your departure. You have no idea where the journey will take you. Still, God hasn't left you the option to stay behind. You have to go and leave with the rest of Israel. You will need to leave your previous life behind and learn how to live a new lifestyle. You will have to learn how to live free. You will need to leave most of the stuff you accumulated in slavery behind as well, but don't be afraid—most of that stuff will be replaced. God will replace your old stuff with good stuff!

Your enemy will have to pay you back wages, and then some. When you leave you will take the treasures denied you in the past. You will leave with treasure that you will need in the days ahead. Be careful though; don't let the treasure become your focus and motivate you! It is just a tool needed for a future time. Yet save a lot of extra room. Start dreaming of your freedom. Begin living your life as though you are already free. Start declaring to all around you that your God will soon be coming for you. Let all those around you know that weeping may last for the night, but joy will come in the morning. When God comes, the morning will break on a brand new life!

Get excited! Get your family ready. Be ready when God calls. We are about to be delivered. We are about to be set free by the God of all creation. We are about to leave. We are about to have a new life handed to us as we leave slavery behind. We are entering a new life where

God is our King. We are beginning a new life where God manifests His abundant care for us!

Father:

I wait for Your deliverance. I declare to all that You are the authority in my life. You are responsible for me. You are the one who cares for me. No force has the right to come near me without Your approval. I come to You Lord Jesus and I will live my life in Your presence. Where You go, I will go. Where You stop, I will stop. I will live in the sanctuary You have created for me. Lord, I am ready to leave this land! Come Quickly Lord Jesus!

CHAPTER

4

Deliverance: Breaking the Yoke

Passover Cup #2

The term "deliverance" can invoke passionate emotions and vivid mental images. Most Christians have an opinion regarding deliverance, its relevance for today and how it takes place. In addition, many Christians have a horror story to tell regarding deliverance. Too many have seen Christian efforts to bring deliverance as harming rather than helping. Still other Christians are oblivious to the effects of evil. They are totally unaware of the price for sin being paid around them. For them, deliverance is a thing of the past even though our Lord clearly taught us to pray for deliverance.

Many problems related to deliverance can be directly tied to our views of the demonic and our relationship to evil. Far too often, Christians have focused too much attention on the power of evil. Many have been taught so much regarding the power of evil that they live in fear. They are told things like, "Don't mess with that demon. It is too big and will eat you alive. Don't go into that building. It was used for devil worship. And don't talk to that person. The demons are too strong."

Some Christians live in a fantasy world where demons can be found around every corner. When the demonic is given more attention than God, strange things can happen. People begin to live in a world focused on the fight against demonic forces and neglect their place of authority and power, living at the throne of God. We can easily forget that we are ambassadors of heaven, under the authority and direction of God. We, all too often, try to do things ourselves and in our own power. And because we have given the demonic so much attention and attempt to exercise authority without submission to God, we cast demons out of anything and everything including our pets. Christians can be seen blaming demons for every problem they encounter. There is no understanding of the relationship between sin and the demonic, and little understanding of the role of God's people in this world.

While some Christians are over-emphasizing the role and power of evil, other Christians refuse to acknowledge the reality of the demonic in our lives. Often, these believers relegate deliverance to out of control demon chasers. These people have little understanding of the reality of evil in this world, or clue as to their role in fighting it. They believe that since Christ defeated the demons at Calvary there is, therefore, no demonic presence in the world today. While that is partly true, these people fail to understand how the defeat of the demonic is playing out on Planet Earth. Even though the Lord has done everything necessary for the defeat of evil, He waits at the side of the Father until all enemies have been placed under His feet. Yet these Christians ignore the reality of evil in front of them and live in a fantasy world.

Unfortunately, we have not only abandoned biblical authority regarding evil and deliverance in the church today, but common sense as well. This allows Christians to ignore the lack of fruit in their live while staunchly defending a way of thinking that doesn't even make sense.

The Apostle Paul admonishes the church to be innocent of evil in the book of Romans. The Lord Jesus warned the church not to learn the deep things of Satan in the Revelation. Today, we must understand that we have no relationship with evil. Our relationship is with the King of kings, who rules over evil. Evil must bow before Christ Jesus. When the church is innocent of evil and excellent at what is good, demonic power is placed in proper perspective. Just as an innocent child has nothing to fear with Daddy around, trusting the parent to handle the evil in and around them, there should be little attention given to the power of evil.

Does God really care for me? Is He interested in intervening in my life to deliver me? Another big issue that hinders many Christians from asking God for deliverance is unbelief. We can easily believe that God will care for our neighbor, yet believing that God actually cares for me is another matter. As a result, we begin looking for relief from other sources. We seek for some magical process that will bring us our freedom, or a special person with the perfect words to answer our dilemmas. "If only I could find a person who has walked here before, they could tell me what to do." We tend to complicate things that are really very simple. If we need deliverance and freedom we should simply ask Him. After asking, we should wait for Him, and we should wait on Him!

Our attempts to find the right process for deliverance has given rise to many different deliverance type ministries. Each one has its own unique approach to deliverance and freedom. While many are teaching sound biblical principles, others teach a process of deliverance that is devoid of God, having no biblical precedent for its patterns or processes. There is no confession of sin and, therefore, no true relief for the burdened. The service they offer provides a mere bandage to cover the bloody mess evil has created. Others are running around the church world selling themselves as uniquely called and anointed of God, to deliver others from the demonic. These people honestly believe that they have something special unavailable to everyone else. This is a dangerous fallacy. Galatians 5:22-23 states:

> *"But the fruit of the Spirit is love, joy, peace, longsuffering, gentleness, goodness, faith, meekness, temperance: against such there is no law."*

In 1 Corinthians 12:8-10 we read:

> *"For to one is given by the Spirit the word of wisdom; To another the word of knowledge by the same Spirit; To another faith by the same Spirit; to another the gifts of healings by the same Spirit; To another the working of miracles; to another prophecy; to another discerning of spirits; to another diverse kinds of tongues; to another the interpretation of tongues..."*

1 Corinthians 12:28 states:

> *"And God hath set some in the church, first apostles, secondarily prophets, thirdly teachers, after that miracles, then gifts of healings, helps, governments, diversity of tongues."*

Finally, Ephesians 4:11 states:

> *"And He gave some, apostles; and some prophets; and some, evangelists; and some, pastors and teachers..."*

These four texts outline various functions within the church, the Body of Christ. Nowhere in these verses, or any other place in Scripture, for that matter, is there a calling or anointing to a deliverance ministry. Deliverance is not a gift of the Spirit or a church office. God does not call or anoint specific people to deliver others from the grasp of evil or demons. God has given every Christian authority over the demonic. God expects that authority to be exercised at His command and in His timing, by any of His children as He directs. God is the deliverer. That is why we ask Him to deliver us from evil. As we walk with God we are given the opportunity to be a part of His miraculous work, to see and be a part of the wondrous authority of Christ Himself.

With so many different views of deliverance and so many different sources available for deliverance today, attempting to find relief can become discouraging. I know one elderly man who was given a death sentence by his doctors. They told him that he would die from a chronic heart problem within five years. There was no possible way he could avoid it. There was no treatment or cure. He was in a desperate situation and no one could offer any type of solution. In addition to the health issues, this man also (admittedly) had baggage in his life that needed to be discarded. There were deep wounds in his life that affected how he lived. Many of the people around him believed that the emotional and physical problems were related. There were many opinions about his situation. Yet what could he do?

One day a friend suggested that a nationally recognized deliverance ministry might be the answer to his troubles. The friend had received some healing from the organization and believed the man would find both a spiritual and physical healing there as well. The friend even offered to pay the three hundred dollar fee, required by the organization, for the seminar when it came to town. When the day came to send in the money it was accompanied with a questionnaire to be filled out and enclosed with the check. After the man filled it out and sent it back to the ministry they refused the man's participation in their seminar on health grounds. They told him that he would not be allowed to join the seminar because his heart could not endure their deliverance process. According to this deliverance ministry, in order to be delivered, an individual needed both money in the bank (at least enough to cover their fee) and a strong constitution. The man was refused healing because the deliverance ministry did not want the liability of the man dying at their meeting.

Can you imagine the Lord turning someone away because they might die on Him? Or being so violent in His method of deliverance that it might kill the person it intended to help? How ludicrous! The Lord never feared such things while He walked the earth. He only obeyed what His Father told Him to do, knowing that the Father could be trusted with the details of what He wanted done. He knew that the Father never made mistakes. There would be no accidents or unforeseen problems. The resources necessary for the job would always be there.

When God delivers, He often defies our logic. Most of the ways of God defy our way of thinking. For example, consider the command given to church leadership to pray for the sick. Not only is an elder in the church required to pray for the sick, he must lay hands on the sick person (Mark 6:18, James 5:14). Now most reasonable persons know that sick people are contagious and we should therefore avoid touching them. Yet God tells elders to touch the sick. To me that makes no sense. If someone is sick I don't want to be around him or her, let alone lay my hands on the person. Yet God commands us to lay hands on the sick. So in obedience, we do it.

As a church, we have laid our hands on people with a variety of problems. Some people have been plagued with major diseases while others have had simple colds or flu. One Sunday a young man came to church and was throwing up all during the service. Afterwards he came forward requesting prayer for his condition. To my surprise, six people came forward and laid their hands on the man and prayed for him. Of the six people who prayed for the man, not one got sick. No one, who had direct contact with the virus, developed the illness.

All of the years that we have laid hands on the sick, I have never seen anyone get sick by laying hands on and praying for them. This defies common sense. Yet God's ways often do not make sense. Often deliverance defies reason as well. Yet when we join God in what He is doing, we can trust Him to handle all the details. We might have done things differently. However, everything will work out for good. We will look back on the process and be amazed at the greatness of God.

One summer we planned a retreat focusing on tearing down the walls that separate us from God. We invited a couple to lead the retreat that lived a walk with the Lord, that we admired. The teaching was excellent, the fellowship good, and the times of worship awesome. Yet every now and then a demonic presence would manifest itself. Just when we thought the retreat was settling down another demonic presence would rise up. Then several deliverances began to occur, with one life after another being changed forever. After a while, we stopped counting the number of deliverances. When a demon would manifest itself, we would continue to spend more time in worship. Needless to say, we spent a lot of time at that retreat in worship.

We were amazed and astounded at the way in which the deliverances were taking place, and asked this couple to explain what they did to instigate so many deliverances. We were looking for them to give us a list of things we could do so that the events of the retreat could be duplicated. Their answer was not what we were looking for. They told us that they weren't doing anything! They hadn't repeated some magical incantation or followed a prescribed list of do's and don'ts. God had merely set the stage for the deliverances, and they were given the opportunity to be a part of what God was doing. They viewed their role in the deliverances as making certain that no one was physically hurt while the demons left. They soothed and calmed the person being delivered, thus, preventing the demonic presence from causing physical damage to the person while leaving.

Today many Christians are in need of deliverance. And far too many Christians lack a basic understanding of God's heart for their freedom. Perhaps, the reason for this is that we have established a life and a form of religion that can exist without God. The Lord Jesus taught us to pray that God would "deliver us from evil." We should allow Him, therefore, to fill that role in our lives once again. We need to stop trying to figure out which demon is attacking us, or why we are being attacked, and instead, bow the knee to the One who can save the soul.

Deliverance is the children's bread; it belongs to the people of God. It is true that Scripture records instances of those who were not children of God being set free from the demonic. However, this is the exception, not the rule. Deliverance from evil belongs to the child of God, by right. Evil dominates the lives of those living away from God. It has a place in these people's lives by their own permission. People invite the demonic through their actions, and by living outside the will and sovereignty of God. In order to be made free, therefore, a person must give

God His rightful place. And that means that a person must be in a relationship with Him.

God has a plan and a process for bringing people from bondage to freedom. It is time for the body of Christ to start walking in that plan. Far too often, when interacting with the unsaved, we attempt to remove the evil in their lives without bringing them to the cross. We often don't realize that when we move outside of God's plan we open doors to trouble. If we truly loved the person who needs deliverance we would bring them into a relationship with God, so that He might become their deliverer.

My wife and I were once invited to join a prominent national ministry for an evening. The woman who led the ministry told us that her focus was on bringing Jesus to the "New Age" culture. She had been actively working to gain the acceptance of New Age people and that night she hoped to be able to boldly share her faith with them. When the evening came we walked into a local New Age worship center. From the names of the angelic gods figured around the room, it was apparent that they worshipped angels. In one corner of the room, the gods of the ages lined the table, including some Catholic holy water, and a very twisted picture of Jesus. They acknowledged Jesus as a god. Jesus to them was just one of many spirit guides. These people were very happy to receive Christians and their ministry as one of many valid and viable ministry alternatives.

When the time of ministry came, the lady, along with her pastor and his wife, began to sing and prophesy over her New Age friends, under the power of her spirit guide, Jesus. These three prophesied the blessings of God over these acknowledged witches, sitting in what was called the "chair of honor." The New Agers loved it and rocked in their seats as if they were in a good church service. They also wept, genuinely grateful for touching the power they called Jesus. They stood in line to get into the chair of honor and received the word of God spoken into their lives. Yet there was no turning from evil. In fact, those ministering never spoke to them about their need to turn from sin and be restored to a relationship with the power they were enjoying that evening.

CHAPTER 4

The evening closed with a couple of witches inviting our friend to sit in the chair of honor. They then began to do a demonic rendition of, what is known in the church as, "speaking in tongues" and prophesying over her, as she had done that evening. They shared their visions of her bright future and told her that her struggles were now coming to an end. A demonic blessing was pronounced over her life. The lady then acknowledged the demonic blessing given to her and actually thanked them for it! She confirmed the blessing and told the witches that she had been given the same message earlier by an Indian medicine man. While all of these things were unfolding her young pastor and his wife were sitting with smiles on their faces, completely oblivious to what had just taken place in the spirit. Afterwards, the young pastor and his wife were excited about having been able to minister their God-given spiritual gifts to the unsaved, even though the gifts of God had just been prostituted and the pastoral office cheapened. There were no lives changed that evening. No one saw the sovereignty of God and bowed their knee to Him. God was placed in the same arena as the Egyptian gods; His authority was compromised before powers that knew He was God.

We are paying a steep price in the church today because of our lack of understanding regarding God's process of freedom. We are playing with evil. It is time for the Body of Christ to stop playing ministry games and start walking under the authority of Heaven. It is time that we began conducting ourselves as ambassadors rather than lovers. And it is time to let love take the form of truth rather than a twisted view of acceptance. We must acknowledge that we need God to change our world, and we must cry out to God that He would heal our land, rebuke the evil that holds us, and move in His power to undo the bonds of sin. It is time to stop thinking more highly of ourselves than we ought, and bow the knee before God, allowing Him to ordain our steps.

What Is True Deliverance and How Does It Occur?

True deliverance is the separation of a person from evil, as well as from their past way of life, along with everything associated with it. The yoke of the former life is broken. When deliverance occurs, life is never the same. The old ways of conduct will be changed forever. There is no turning back to the old lifestyle because the old life doesn't exist anymore. Any path that might lead back to the old life has been cut off. The person is not welcome in Egypt anymore. When the word of deliverance is spoken the person becomes like an individual without a country - literally "between lands." They have been rejected by Egypt, yet they have not left for the Promised Land. The old life is gone. Now we must move on to the new life!

Deliverance is not a long drawn out process. Deliverance occurs with one decree, "Go and worship your God!" Evil will not wait for the morning light to send us on our way. The decree granting our release will be immediate, while the wounds are still fresh. As soon as the decree is made, we are on our way! It is now time to assemble with God's people. God is now personally leading and directing. Our new life has just begun.

Lead on, Oh King!

CHAPTER

5

The Road to Redemption

Once deliverance has taken place, it is time to leave the land. Pharaoh has temporarily released his hold and God has called a gathering. Pharaoh has allowed God the right to rule Israel, and that right will never be relinquished. From now on God, not Pharaoh, will be calling the shots, leading and directing His people. That does not mean that the tie with Egypt is completely broken. Pharaoh may still claim ownership of the people of Israel. Nevertheless, the journey begins which will bring a permanent change of ownership, from Pharaoh to God. Redemption must come so that Israel will permanently understand that they have been "bought with a price."

In a certain sense, it appears as if God has backed Himself into a corner. He has told Israel one thing, and Pharaoh another. How then will He get out of this dilemma? While Israel is expecting to leave Egypt forever, Moses has only asked Pharaoh for permission to travel a three-day journey into the desert to worship. Israel is expecting to be totally free from Egypt. Egypt, on the other hand, is expecting Israel to return after their worship time in the desert is completed.

So you see the stakes are extremely high, stretching far beyond the honor of God. Telling Pharaoh one thing, and Israel another, could have had enormous implications. If God's words were not true (to either Israel or Pharaoh) the very existence of the world would have been in jeopardy. That's because both its origins and continued existence are dependent on one thing: the veracity of God's Word. Therefore, if the world is to continue, God's word to Israel and Pharaoh must be accurate. If it's not, the world itself might fall apart and cease to exist, including mankind.

God is working on two fronts in order to transfer ownership of Israel completely to Himself. On one front He is actively leading Israel. As far as Israel is concerned, they are free to follow their God. They have no thought of ever returning to Egypt and slavery. Yet on another front, God is dealing with Pharaoh and Egypt, masterfully aligning Egypt to violate its own contract and, therefore, bring about its own destruction. God is directing Israel's movements and this incites Egypt to move out. While His people stand under His rule, He is preparing Egypt to attack them. Yet every move God directs Israel to make, prepares them to be redeemed.

The change of permanent ownership will come, and the people will be bought back by God. Egypt will attack, but they will be totally defeated. Israel will begin the journey which will prepare them to rule in their own land as God's people. But first, Egypt must be set up for a fall. The preparation for redemption includes Israel visiting four Egyptian cities: four stops in order to get the world off their back. They are Rameses, Succoth, Etham, and Migdol.

Rameses

Rameses was the treasure city of Egypt where many of the riches of the Pharaohs were stored. It was also the gathering place for Israel. Found in the northeastern area of Egypt by the Nile delta, Rameses was in the land of Goshen. It is here in Goshen that Jacob settled when he first came to Egypt, and, eventually, Goshen became Israel's home for four hundred years. Rameses was also the location of Israel's last slave labor project for Pharaoh.

It is in Rameses that Egypt finally compelled Israel to leave their land, after the death of their firstborn. Every firstborn, whether human or animal, was destroyed from every household in Egypt that was not protected by God. The loss of the firstborn had capped a long string of losses for the Egyptians. Egypt was reeling from the ravaging of their land and desperate to get rid of Israel. By the time the Passover night had run its course, Egypt was convinced that if they did not release Israel to worship God all of the remaining Egyptians would die as well! The Egyptians knew that the God of Israel was standing against them.

Yet while Egypt was desperate to rid themselves of Israel, a change was taking place within the people of God. They were beginning to learn to relate to God as a group. Prior to the Passover there had been no interaction between God and the Israelites in Egypt. On the evening of Passover they began to have intimate contact with God, at least on an individual family basis. But they were now to learn how to relate to God as a nation as well. They would see the hand of God, experience His wonders, know His provision, and follow His leading as a group. Their war with Pharoah was not yet finished; there were still dangers to face. Yet this peril must now be faced as a group, and not merely on an individual basis. From now on, Israel would interact with God as a nation.

This group of former slaves now gathered at Rameses, turning their attention to the Egyptians. They went door to door asking the Egyptians to give up their silver, gold, and clothing. This plundering of Egypt, far from an ordinary event, was an incredible feat. The mightiest nation on earth now voluntarily gave its wealth to a race of former slaves. Israel had only to go to Egypt's door and ask, and all the riches of Egypt was theirs. They came out of slavery with incredible wealth. Whatever the people of God asked for, the Egyptians gave without question.

Once the decree of deliverance is sounded our world begins to change, just as Israel's world changed. God places us within the Body of Christ, and that is where He begins to relate to us. We begin to discover that we are not the only one who loves God, but are part of a greater whole. We find strength in being a part of the group. No longer do we have to face anything alone. Our walk with God now involves other people. We begin to learn together, walk together, and relate to God together.

Every time God brings His deliverance, we gain a greater understanding of our own place within the Body of Christ. We also gain a better understanding of who God has invited us to be. Our specific destiny, established by God from the beginning of time, comes into clearer focus.

Learning to take our place within the Body of Christ brings fulfillment. No longer do we have to wander around wondering how we fit in, or sit on the outside looking in. God has given us a place and it is good. Every time we endure a little more refining, we are given a little more understanding of why we were created. As we live out our destiny, we are made to feel complete. We begin to see what role we are playing in the Kingdom of God, and how our life is pleasing to God. What more could we ask for? Life is good! For Israel their first assignment after their deliverance was to gather resources. The tasks ahead were going to require tools and resources that Israel did not have, since it was taken away from them during their slavery.

It is no different today. Evil is still a thief. The Lord described Satan and his forces in the following way, "The thief cometh not, but for to steal, and to kill, and to destroy... (John 10:10)." When we are slaves to evil, our life is sucked away. Our resources are stolen or even destroyed, including our health, money, relationships, peace of mind, time, freedom, etc. Evil wants us dead and will not stop until we are of no possible threat to the kingdom of darkness.

Yet after the decree of deliverance is made, it is time to approach our former captors and politely ask for their wealth. It is time to stand at their front door and announce that we are there for the wealth. This principle may seem strange. Yet we must have resources necessary to accomplish what God has called us to do. If you are married and your spouse has been held by evil, it has prevented you from fulfilling and enjoying the marriage relationship God has designed. When deliverance comes to your spouse, you are delivered as well. You now have the right to extract from evil the wealth necessary to fulfill the task God has given you in your marriage. You can demand that evil provide extra time and money to develop your relationship with your spouse. The same is true regarding money. If God's destiny for you is to provide money for His Kingdom and evil has stolen your business, you can approach evil and demand, "Give me your money!" Doesn't that sound exciting?

Succoth

The children of Israel left Rameses and traveled to Succoth. At Succoth they picked up the bones of Joseph and marched on in battle array to Etham. These actions by Israel had a profound impact on their relationship with Pharaoh. Because of this sojourn at Succoth, their entire world was about to change. They probably had no realization of what impact these simple actions would have on their lives. All of Egypt would be in an uproar because of this one stop.

We should remember that Succoth was the place in the land of Goshen where Jacob settled when he came to Egypt. Here in Succoth, Jacob pitched his tent (which is where the name Succoth comes from). Succoth was also the place where the body of Joseph was entombed. Joseph had made Israel promise to take his body back to the Promised Land when they left. This promise was well known in the courts of Pharaoh. As a result, when Pharaoh heard the news that the body of Joseph had been picked up, He was furious. Pharaoh realized that Israel was attempting to escape Egypt rather than merely worship for a while in the desert. Pharaoh gathered his armies with the sole purpose of retaking Israel and bringing them back to slavery. The sign to Pharaoh that Israel was leaving was the empty tomb of Joseph. Evil would be tricked into losing its rights over God's people by an empty tomb!

Sound familiar? The same pattern would repeat itself fifteen hundred years later. This time the sign that God's people were soon to be free was nothing less than the empty tomb of Jesus! Evil was once again duped by an empty tomb.

Pharaoh heard of the empty tomb of Joseph and mobilized Egypt to retake Israel. This would prove to be a fatal blunder. If Pharaoh had any idea as to the honor and majesty of God, he would have stayed in his palace. If he had stayed home, God's honor and integrity would have brought Israel back to Egypt. Pharaoh could have received his slaves back without any further trouble or bloodshed, and Moses' request to worship in the desert would have been fulfilled. Israel would have returned to Egypt peaceably. But Pharaoh's heart had been hardened, and Egypt was bent on recapturing Israel. Pharaoh did not realize that was he was about to attack Israel while they were under the protection of God. Yet he was playing into the hand of God and was about to bring on his own destruction. Who would dare to attack people who are under the protection of God?

Israel was oblivious to the events in Pharaoh's court and had no idea that Pharaoh was on his way to get them. They were merely following the direction of God by fulfilling the request of Joseph. They had no clue that their actions at Succoth would create such a stir in the courts of Pharaoh.

The reality of the principles revealed at Succoth has sounded out throughout the centuries. These principles were evident during the events surrounding the death and resurrection of the Lord. The reality of Succoth can be seen in our own lives as well. Someday the full impact of them will be applied to the whole earth with the defeat of evil and death. The basic principle of Succoth is that God always causes evil to bring about its own destruction. Like Ahab who was tricked to fight in a battle that would cause his death, or Satan who conspired to kill the Lord and bring about his own demise, God always sets up evil for a fall. In our lives God uses seemingly innocent actions to force powers and principalities into releasing their hold on us. Evil will lose its hold on us permanently because of its own foolish responses to an act of God. God will continue to use an empty tomb to bring His people freedom!

The arrogance of evil is that it wants to be like God, exercising his authority to reign. This arrogance was first seen with Satan in the Garden of Eden and was eventually passed on to Adam and Eve. Since that time, like a plague, it has been passed down throughout the race. Yet evil's desires do not detract in the slightest from God's sovereignty. While many peoples and powers claim to be god, no claim has ever moved God off of His throne. That's because He always sets up arrogance to destroy itself.

The power evil possesses is stolen and temporary. That is why God always takes action when arrogance stands against the rule of God. Yet such action is seldom direct. God's usual approach to removing the authority of evil is to trick it into destroying itself. This was the case in Egypt, as well as during the time of Israel in the Promised Land. It was supremely true during the defeat of evil, by the Lord, at the cross and in the empty tomb. This fact will bear out when evil is dealt the final blow and a new heaven and earth are established.

When Pharaoh and the forces of Egypt saw God's people living as though the word of God had already been accomplished, they broke their contract with Israel. They were marching as though they were already free of Pharaoh. Picking up the bones of Joseph was a physical sign of this attitude and lifestyle. Though they were not yet free and their redemption had not yet come, still their actions told Pharaoh that Israel was leaving forever. Pharaoh reacted to something that had not happened yet.

A basic definition of faith is that we live as if God's word will come to pass (no matter what). When we do live that way, as if the reality of God's spoken word is already here, we are living in faith. Evil then responds to our faith (even though nothing has changed in the physical). Evil brings about its own doom because we begin living in the reality of God's word rather than what we see around us.

We do not understand all the mysteries of God. The truth is, we often have a difficult time understanding the most basic leadings of God in our lives. Yet God will bring us to a place where our actions will force the hand of evil. As a result, the permanent hold of evil will be removed from our lives. Our former relationship with evil and the trouble it caused will become a memory that gradually fades into the past.

Most likely, we will not understand why God is leading in a certain direction or how our actions will force the hand of evil. In fact, if we did know the results of our actions and the trouble it would cause we probably would not do what we were asked to do. If we knew where we were going and what would be encountered, we probably wouldn't go. God knows what is best for us. We will know soon enough the ramifications of our stop at Succoth. Until then, we keep marching in battle array.

Etham

Welcome to Etham! Etham means "rock". One would not think a desert place like Etham to be worthwhile or noteworthy. Yet Israel's stop here at Etham shaped the relationship between God and Israel for the next forty-two years. This stop determined how Israel would perceive God until they crossed into the Promised Land. In the place of the rock, God defined how Israel would see Him. Here at Etham, the manifest presence of God was given to the children of Israel.

God had taken charge of Israel at Rameses. At Succoth, evil's destruction was set in motion. Now at Etham, visible signs of God's direction were given to Israel. By day a pillar of cloud was before them, and by night a pillar of fire could be seen. An unexplainable, supernatural sign hung, undeniably, in front of the camp. These pillars would be continually before them until Israel left the wilderness. Every Bible story from this point until Joshua crosses the Jordan took place with the manifest presence of God. It became the backdrop for all Israelite activities in the wilderness. A day did not go by where the Israelites did not see the manifest presence of God.

No Israelite could deny that the God of Abraham, Isaac, and Jacob was guiding their path and was fully in charge. There could be no murmuring in the background. No one could wonder if Moses was responsible to lead the people. If they had a problem with their situation or circumstances they had only one source to blame or complain to: God. At least it seemed to be that simple.

Israel's task in following God was not difficult. They merely had to

CHAPTER 5

look up to perceive the supernatural leading of God. They did not wonder if God really existed. Nor could they question whether or not God was responsible for bringing them to this point. There could be no second-guessing the events in Egypt. God was with them. From this point on, Israel must stay with Him. When the pillar moved, they must move along with it. They had no idea where the pillar would lead them; if they had known they probably would not have gone. Their job was to stay with God, letting Him worry about the path they were on and its details.

The gathering of God's people is complete. The oppressor has filled the pockets and carts with wealth. The bones of Joseph have been picked up. Now where do we go? Look up! God is going to take personal responsibility for the path ahead. God will give us His manifest presence to guide us in the days ahead. When God begins to lead us supernaturally, there is no doubt or second-guessing. We may not have all the answers or understand everything that is going on, but we know that God is leading us away from Egypt. We know that we are in the right place.

Today God continues to bring His people to Etham. At Etham, He makes His presence known and gives clear direction to His people. Throughout the remainder of the process leading to freedom and the ensuing training that follows, there is never a question as to the reality or presence of God. God will be with His people. Knowing where He is and where He is going is not difficult. All that we need to do is to simply look up! At the Rock, we will find peace that can only be found in God and that will guide and direct us forever. It is a peace which guarantees us that the sovereign God is in control of our lives. Such a peace will never let us go.

We don't know where He is going to lead us or what lies ahead. If we did know where God was taking us, we would probably wonder if we signed up for the right tour. By now it is a fair bet that evil is on its way, and that the process of redemption has been set in motion. Only God can pull off what is to follow. He alone has the strength to complete what is ahead. At this point, He knows where we are going and why. God is protecting us from encountering enemies that can't be handled. If we had even the slightest hint as to what was ahead we would not want to go. Yet, even though we do not have all the information, we must follow Him. There is no other alternative for us. We must look up and follow God wherever He may lead us, fully trusting Him. We must trust that He will lead, protect, and defend us.

Migdol

Migdol means "the tower", and is the last place on earth we would want to be with Pharaoh hot on our heels. At the bottom corner of the Sinai Peninsula, the Gulf of Acaba is on one side with the Red Sea on another, and a lot of desert in front of us. Pharaoh and his armies will be closing in from the desert, which leaves no visible means of escape. We are trapped in the corner with few alternatives: fight the superior forces of Egypt on their own terms, role over and die, or surrender and return to Egypt and slavery. None of these alternatives seem desirable to newly freed slaves with their pockets full of Egyptian gold and silver. It is beginning to look as though Israel will die at the hands of Pharaoh's armies with their families at their side.

Defenseless, helpless, and vulnerable best describe the situation. There is no place to hide or establish a good defense, nor any place to go. There is no fleet of boats to launch a rescue. There is nothing that can be done to prepare for the onslaught of Pharaoh. Israel can march in battle array all they want. They can sharpen spears night and day, yet no amount of effort will prevent the upcoming slaughter or change the outcome of battle. Israel is physically mismatched in every category. They don't have a chance!

By now the entire camp of Israel would have known that Pharaoh was on his way. Their attempts at aligning in battle array would seem a waste of time now. No matter how fierce Israel may look, she is no match for the armies of Egypt. Their doom was set, or so it seemed. The only option before Israel now is to wait for Pharaoh to show up. They must wait and see what will happen and if God can be trusted. Will redemption come or will it be their destruction?

Just before redemption comes into our lives, God places us in an impossible spot. We have followed Him faithfully, yet He has led us to the corner of nowhere. We can't imagine why God would bring us to such a vulnerable area. Then, to our surprise, we learn that God is leading our worst enemy straight to us. That enemy is angry and looking for blood. We are completely unprepared for battle. There isn't enough time to prepare for the coming slaughter. Even if we knew what to do, we couldn't do it. There is nothing we can do but wait - either for our own destruction or our salvation. Which will it be; life or death? How could God allow the enemy to gain the upper hand? Why is the enemy here at all? Why must we face the same enemy that we left behind in Egypt?

The stage is now set for redemption. The players are in place for the permanent ownership change of God's people. Soon Pharaoh will see why it is not a good idea to attack the people of God when He is protecting them. Soon God's people will know true freedom, not just the absence of evil. Soon they will know what it means to be owned by God.

Father:

You now are in control. Lead me where You wish. Give me the words and the courage to gather the resources necessary for the tasks ahead. Open the tombs before me and lead according to Your great designs. Grant to me Your manifest presence to guide me throughout this journey. Lord, grant me Your peace to bring calm in the midst of the storm. Bring me to Your place of freedom. Bring me to the place where Your name will be exalted.

CHAPTER

6

Redemption: A Change of Ownership

Passover Cup #3

"The building needs a new roof." That is what we were told when we bought a church facility to house our congregation. We had been meeting in a school gymnasium for five and a half years, and the prospect of moving into any church building sounded great to us. In addition, the building was in an impoverished area of our city. We couldn't have asked for more. Now, we could take our place as a church in our city.

We had been told that the roof needed new shingles and that all the new shingles had been donated. We were also told that a general contractor was waiting in the wings to donate the labor necessary to replace the roof. Even if the contractor failed us, most of our congregation was young so we were able to do the work ourselves. Or so we thought.

We were then told that the building had been severely damaged and was in need of extensive repair. Our simple re-shingling job was becoming a major reconstruction project that was far out of our grasp. Instead of adding a new layer of shingles, three older roofs needed to be removed. In addition, a full third of the roof trusses needed to be taken out and replaced. Our free re-roofing was turning into a major effort that our people could not physically do. In all, our free roof job now had a price tag of over $175,000. We barely made our meager budget every month. Raising an additional $175,000 was impossible. Even if we felt debt was a viable alternative, we couldn't afford to borrow that kind of money. We would never be able to afford the payments.

Now the roof became our enemy. When ice backed up it rained in the church. When it rained, every area of the church got wet. If I kept anything in my office it eventually would get wet. We had mop buckets strategically placed around the church to prevent small puddles from completely ruining already moldy stained carpet. We were becoming discouraged and were losing hope. Every bit of energy was being poured into this distressed building. We couldn't seem to get past the building to focus on being a light to our new neighborhood. The building was supposed to be there to serve us. Instead, it was preventing us from doing what we were called to do.

The cost to repair the building was beyond anything we could afford. There was no way we could raise the money from within the congregation, and we didn't know enough people outside the congregation who were willing to help either. All we could do was watch the rain continue to pour into the building.

We knew that God had placed us in this building, as well as in that neighborhood, to make a difference. We knew that we were in the plan of God and that He had prepared the way for us to be where we were. His manifest presence had never left. Yet we wondered where His provision was. Didn't God know that the roof was falling in on us and that we needed Him to move on our behalf? Were we missing something? Were demonic forces preventing us from coming into God's plan for us?

One Sunday, I stood before the congregation and announced that this was our "Red Sea" experience. This was a time in our church's life where either God would move on our behalf or else we would die. There was no middle ground. We would either survive the onslaught of the building or we would disband as a church. The prospect of complete failure was a very real possibility. Not only did we face the physical challenges of the building, but the spiritual challenges were overwhelming too. The last two congregations in the same building had disbanded with one pastor leaving the ministry altogether, totally burned out.

One day the winds blew through town at a rate of over seventy miles per hour and took a portion of our roof off the building. I could not believe my eyes! "What's next?" I thought. How could we ever deal with this problem? The outlook was bleak, at best. Yet the ripping off of the roof was the beginning of our old building's redemption. Within a few weeks, our insurance company paved the way for us to begin a new roof project. Within a few more weeks, three of our congregation's families came into an inheritance and each family gave a portion to the roof project. We were on our way. However, we would soon find out what being at the Red Sea was all about. We had the opportunity to see first hand how God buys back what belongs to Him. Through the plans and trials of a building project, we would learn how to endure.

Israel at the Red Sea

At the Red Sea, Israel was backed into the corner of the Sinai Peninsula with nowhere to go. They had no allies to call on. They faced certain doom with no possibility of success against a superior enemy. And that enemy was angry, wanting their total destruction.

The appointed time arrived. The stage was set for redemption, and all the players were on stage as the curtain went up. Pharaoh and the Egyptians caught up with Israel at Migdol. Israel was now boxed in with their former oppressors staring them in the face. On both sides of them they were surrounded by water. They were trapped with absolutely nowhere to go and nothing to do! What had started out to look so good for Israel now looked like certain defeat. Must Israel face Egypt again? Weren't they already delivered from Pharaoh? Why, then, did God bring them to this defenseless place? Israel was once again facing the onslaught of Egypt.

This time, however, things were different. The last time Egypt confronted Israel they were slaves who were already completely dominated by them. The only lifestyle Israel knew was Egyptian. They had not yet been invited into a relationship with God. All they really knew was the whip of the oppressor. Now things were different. Israel may now be facing danger, but at least they were out of Egypt. Though they may be facing certain destruction, they were now standing with their God.

In Egypt, Israel saw their oppressors from the perspective of a person bowed before their taskmaster. They saw evil from the perspective of those completely dominated by that evil. In the desert, though, with God leading them, the perspective was much different. Of course, the same evil had returned, but now it was on the outside trying to get in (not on the inside ruling). The children of Israel now saw evil from God's perspective. They saw evil trying desperately to reassert its dominion over a soon-to-be-free people. Pharaoh and his armies looked totally overwhelming.

Israel was almost removed from the process as God took charge of the next encounter with Egypt. Israel's role was limited to being an observer in the final battle between God and the king of Egypt. This conflict would determine Israel's future, yet Israel would play no role in the battle. They were on the outside of the trouble as God entered the field of battle.

There was Pharaoh, with superior military forces, revered and feared throughout the region and the world. Yet he had no idea of the gross misjudgment he had made. His arrogance was about to get a lot of people killed. Pharaoh had given Israel the right to go into the desert to worship God. Now he was about to break his contract with Israel and God, pitting himself against the power and sovereignty of God Himself! As a result, Pharaoh was about to lose everything.

Israel was about to gain it all, yet she didn't know it. She had no idea that the apparent destruction to be unleashed was their redemption in disguise, and that the destruction they expected from the hand of Pharaoh would never come. Instead, Pharaoh himself would be destroyed. In fact, it would be Pharaoh who would insure their future as children of God. His premature running after Israel would cost him

CHAPTER 6

everything. Israel would benefit beyond their wildest dreams! They could not have imagined what they were soon to see from the hand of God.

Suddenly, Pharaoh was there and night was falling. How does Israel respond? Probably the same way you and I would respond—with fear. They were scared and began talking as though there was no hope. In their fear, they began looking for someone to blame for their situation. What they should have been doing was looking for someone to thank, rather than someone to blame.

Even though God was there at Migdol the people began to mutter and complain. Despite the fact that God had been directing them, they couldn't see past their own fear. Yet God understood the limitations of Israel at the Red Sea. He knew that they had just come out of slavery and were not yet a people of faith. Israel did not yet know how to walk in the ways of God. God didn't punish their unbelief, or remove His manifest presence from Israel. He would, of course, correct their unbelief at a later time. For now, He made one thing very clear: fear was not an option!

It was Israel's fear that tempted them to become participants in God's plan of redemption. This was contrary to God's plan. God never wanted Israel to participate in their own redemption. Israel was to have nothing to do with their own salvation; they could not be trusted in such delicate matters. Just as God put Abraham asleep while making a covenant with Him, God set Israel on the sidelines to watch His redemption unfold before them. All generations would have to acknowledge the sovereign redemption by the God of Abraham, Isaac, and Jacob. God Himself would be given the sole credit for the supernatural events of the day. God wanted Israel to watch their redemption unfold before them. There would be things for them to do later on, but for now their orders were to sit tight and watch the salvation of their God.

The fact that God didn't want Israel involved in the battle with Egypt was evident in that He moved the pillar between Israel and the forces of Egypt. His manifest presence became a shield between Israel and evil. What a brilliant move! On the side of Egypt, darkness enveloped the pursuers so that they could not find Israel. Confusion abounded in the Egyptian camp. As the night progressed, the pursuit of Israel ground to a complete halt. Yet on the other side of the pillar there was light in the nighttime for Israel! Israel could not see the Egyptians, nor could the Egyptians find Israel. In fact, the Egyptians couldn't even find each other! On Israel's side of the pillar, God provided light to allow Israel to work through the night and get to their freedom. Night gave way to day as the people of God prepared to move out in a direction no one could have dreamed of before. Who would have thought an escape route by sea was even an option?

Once Pharaoh was isolated from Israel, God commanded Moses to stretch out his hands over the sea. To the Israelites the result was totally unimaginable. A wind came from across the sea (blowing straight at them out of the east) and the sea split in front of them. Before their very eyes was a road from one peninsula to another with a wall of water on each side. There actually was a way to escape from Pharaoh! Israel just hadn't seen it before.

While they could not have possibly known about this way of escape, God had actually prepared for it thousands of years before Israel's journey to the Red Sea. During the days of Peleg, the earth's continents moved which provided a shelf just below the surface of the water. This shelf connected the Sinai Peninsula with the Arabian Peninsula. On either side of the shelf, the bottom dropped off two thousand feet. God had made a secret road for Israel that He had hidden until this time, a private road that was now being exposed. After all the years of waiting, this part of God's plan of redemption was ready to be revealed. Israel entered the sea as slaves of Pharaoh, but they passed through the waters and emerged on the other side. They watched from a place of safety as God became their new owner. All of Pharaoh's right to the Israelites would be taken over by God.

Prior to this the children of Israel were called the people of God in name only. Israel could only claim the name of God by faith. Yet they knew the time would come when they would become the physical possession of the God of all creation. They would soon be the most unique nation in all the earth. There had never been any nation like them, nor would there ever be another nation like them afterwards. While the rest of the world related to God under a specific set of rules, Israel would relate to God in a completely different manner. They would see God like no other people on the planet.

The wind was blowing out of the east with enough strength to move the water into two walls. Now the command was given to Israel to enter the sea. The way of escape was before them but it was not easy to move ahead because of the force of the winds, which were enough to make walls of water on either side. Even though Israel had been given the command escape through the sea, they still had a lot of work to do. They must fight their way to freedom. There was no way that they could go backwards since Pharaoh was on their heels. Nor could they stay put, for Pharaoh would eventually find them. They must brave the unimaginable by walking under a sea, conquering the winds to get to the other side.

Just as escape seems possible, God does something totally unexpected, which Israel probably didn't appreciate at the time. He removed the pillar that separated them from the Egyptians. Egypt was suddenly able to see Israel, as well as their escape route, and that meant that Egypt could follow them! As night ended and day was beginning to break, Egypt began to pursue Israel. The last thing Israel would have wanted was now happening before their eyes: Pharaoh was chasing after them as they were escaping under the waters.

Israel watched the Egyptians enter the sea from the opposite side of the waters. They entered the sea as slaves, and came out as slaves on the other side. From the other side, Israel watched evil try to follow them, thinking that it could destroy the people of God. But evil was wrong. God looked down through the pillars of His manifest presence and saw Pharaoh trying to attack Israel. Egypt was using God's escape route to get to Israel! But Pharaoh had no business being on the road that had been prepared for Israel's use only. There was no way that evil could play by the same rules as God's people.

It was now time to see the permanent removal of the evil that owned

Israel. As they entered the sea, the lead Egyptian chariots developed wheel trouble and the wheels began to fall off. Soon the entire Egyptian army was abandoning all of their equipment and animals and running as fast as they could back to the shore of the sea. Fear enveloped the army as they frantically tried to get out of the sea. All of Pharaoh's mighty hosts were running scared back to the very shore where they had first entered the sea.

As the armies of Egypt ran back towards Pharaoh, Moses stretched his hands once more over the sea. The sea walls collapsed so that the Egyptians were caught in the sea and instantly destroyed. The Israelites were instantly freed from the threat of Pharaoh and they would never go back again, even if they wanted to. They were freed by an event that they had already walked through. They were freed when evil attempted to follow them through a path designed only for the people of God. Evil lost because it crossed into an area where it had no right to exist. Israel watched God's past provision devour today's problems. Sound a little familiar?

Redemption Today

The meaning of redemption is to "buy back." When God redeems us, He removes the ownership rights of evil and buys us back for Himself. When redemption is finished, we have a new owner; our allegiances, as well as our citizenship are changed forever. We become aligned with a new protector and directed by another force. When redemption is accomplished, we are called children of God and citizens of heaven.

Redemption occurs in every Christian's life once. We are redeemed from the kingdom of darkness and are placed into the Kingdom of God when we first accept God's salvation. Yet redemption happens every day of our lives as well. Throughout our lives, God continues to redeem us for Himself. This continuing redemption will not stop until our bodies have been replaced with a model that will last for all eternity.

When God speaks deliverance into our lives, He declares our freedom from evil in order that we might live unto Him. When God prepares us for redemption, He sets up evil for a fall; a fatal fall, from which it will never recover. Redemption is the sovereign act of God that removes the influence of evil permanently. Yet if we are not familiar with God's ways, we can easily become discouraged when we are standing at the shore of the Red Sea. We can easily confuse purification and redemption, and in so doing, give up at a time when complete victory is so close! Discouragement or fear can cause us to miss the wonders and excitement of God's redemption! A time that could be completely exciting becomes overshadowed by fear, doom, and gloom. While we could be enjoying the drama in front of us, we cower in the corner, hoping for the end to come soon.

So here we are, in the corner of the Sinai Peninsula with the sea behind us on two sides and the open desert before us. It makes no sense to be there in the first place. But then the unheard of is sounded through the camp. In this region that can't be defended, Pharaoh is on his way to undo our deliverance. The same evil from which we were delivered is coming back to us. Will it ever end? We thought we were delivered from that problem already! "Do we need to be delivered again?"

We can relax, since deliverance has already taken place. Purification has done its work and God has declared our freedom. Evil has temporarily released us to the protection of God. God is now making that relationship a permanent one! From our perspective, God became our sole owner at our deliverance. However, God still has some housekeeping to do. Redemption is on its way. We must now wait for evil to cross the line and bring about its own destruction. It is time to watch vulnerability give way to victory. We must become weak so that the strength of the Lord may be revealed. Let evil think it can win... we can stand still and watch as God takes control!

The truth is, God is going to battle as our representative. He will handle the situation for us. Our role in the conflict is simply to watch the salvation of our God. The conflict and the place of battle are not pretty and it's not fun to be here, yet the problems and issues have been taken over by God. Our time by the sea is going to be limited. Truly, the situation in front of us isn't our problem at all; it is God's! He has taken responsibility... it is His battle.

During the darkest hours of our roof project, many people thought it would be the death of our church. It had been the death of the churches that were in the building before us. The neighborhood had seen one failed church after another. Death and destruction were an expected part of life. The curses were strong and so was the evil to be rebuked. As a church, we should have known that redemption was going to be a big deal. When redemption was brought to our little corner of the neighborhood, the battle would be huge and very visible.

Some churches in our area talked encouragingly, as did some wealthy individuals from outside the church. Yet apart from a token gift here and there, we faced our potential doom alone. Interestingly, nobody in the church was excited about this. Nobody stood up and declared our redemption was at hand; at least at first.

We learned through all this that fear is the number one enemy of redemption. Fear makes us do stupid things, such as speaking death when we should be speaking the life of God into our situation. Fear, if left unchecked will interfere with evil's defeat. Instead of dealing with the evil, God will have to turn His attention to dealing with us. If we understand that fear is our number one enemy during redemption, we can be on the lookout for it. When it shows up we are not surprised, and, therefore, know what to do: be quiet!

For many of us the idea of being quiet is something new. We are usually trying to find something to do or say. Yet, in redemption, God wants us out of the picture. Our number one enemy during the process is best dealt with through inaction. The next time we encounter fear we must tell it to be quiet. Being quiet is the best thing we can do. Silence dissipates fear and drains its energy. Jesus told us this when he spoke to His disciples:

> "Peace I leave with you, My peace I give unto you: not as the world giveth, give I unto you. Let not your heart be troubled, neither let it be afraid." (John 14:27)

Fear feeds on itself. The more you talk about it, the more it builds. Fear can snowball into a frenzy that starts a downward spiral into an arena of irrational actions. Fear drives people to do crazy things. The only way to deal with it is by standing in front of it and seeing it as irrational, so it can be stopped dead in its tracks. Telling fear to be quiet stops things from getting out of hand.

So when fear tries to short-circuit God's redemptive process in your life, refuse it! Hold your peace and watch the hand of God bring you permanent freedom. Evil is back for a reason; it is about to play into God's hands. Remind yourself that it was God who brought you to this place. He called evil to gather together against you because He has set up your redemption. He can be trusted with the process, as well as the outcome! Even if nothing looks or sounds right, let God have enough space to do what needs to be done. Allow God to work outside your box of understanding to bring an ownership change in your life.

The way in which God provided for the roof project in our church was nothing like what we expected. When the old roof was taken off and a new roof put on, everyone on our side of town watched it. As the curses in the spiritual realm were dealt with, we began to see the physical changed as well. God set our church on the sidelines as He began His work of redemption. Yes, it was tough. First of all, we had to change our way of thinking. Yes, it was a fight, but it was God's fight! When victory came we got to enjoy it with Him.

We will fight the winds as we leave our oppressors behind. We will have to press on against the very thing that is making our way of escape. Yet when redemption is working we have no other alternative. We must press on and get to the other side, pressing through anything that comes against us. We hold on to the word that God has spoken and take the plunge!

Evil wants to undo our deliverance. When the time is ripe for redemption, evil is back! But this time around things are different. Before we were slaves to this evil, serving and fearing it. Now evil doesn't look so powerful as it tries to exert authority back into our lives. It is on the outside trying desperately to get back in. Meanwhile, we are enjoying the manifest presence of God and evil is the anxious one, struggling to regain control. If we keep fear out of the picture we can actually enjoy what is happening and give thanks for it.

During purification we were bowed before evil as we were coming into a relationship with God. Now we have a really special new relationship with God and evil wants back in. But God will not allow it! A battle is going to take place, but God does not want us involved. His manifest presence, which has brought us to this place, is about to light up our lives. God is removing us from the process as He takes full control. Our relationship and interaction is with God Himself. He is about to deal with evil for us. God takes us outside the problem as He takes charge of the solution. To protect us while His plan unfolds, God places His manifest presence between us and the evil. The manifest presence of God becomes a light at night for us, and a wall of darkness to our enemy. God's manifest presence becomes a light in the night to allow us the ability to work through the darkness and accomplish the tasks in front of us.

The manifest presence of God is none other than the Lord Himself. The Lord Jesus Christ, our Messiah, becomes the wall between us and the evil that looks to destroy us. The Lord is, to us, a light to brighten the night - but to evil, He is a shield preventing it from getting to us. As the Lord's presence fills the night, we prepare to move out. We don't know where we are going, nor do we understand any of the events that are taking place. What we do know is that we ought to be in battle with a great army. Instead, we are standing by the shore, holding our stuff as though we are all about to walk on water.

The winds begin to blow, but they are blowing straight at us. There is enough force to take the waters of the sea and turn them into two walls on either side of us. But forward we must go. We fight the winds and begin to cross under the sea. Staying where we are is not an option. Neither is going backwards. We must fight the winds and get to the other side.

Under the waterline, we find ourselves in a type of death. Something in us is dying as we fight the wind to get to the other shore. We fight to get to a new land not controlled by Pharaoh. We are trying to get to a land where we have not been before; to the land called the wilderness, where we will be alone with God, without interference from anyone else. There He can begin to teach us how to rule our Promised Land.

When we come up we will be in another land, in a relationship with God we have not had before. But first, we must make a trip to the cross. An aspect of who we have been must be taken to the place of death, so that it may die with Christ. We will change under the waters. Though we may not understand the change or be able to describe it, we will be different when we come back up. As we come up out of the waters we feel freer, lighter, like we have touched the life of God in a fresh and new way. Who wants the land of Egypt now? We turn our sights towards the wilderness and our hopes towards the Promised Land. There is just one more problem to deal with - Pharaoh is still behind us.

God lifted the screen between evil and ourselves as soon as we entered the sea. Why couldn't God just leave us protected until Pharaoh tired of trying to recapture us and returned to Egypt? Now Pharaoh sees our escape route and where we are going. Evil didn't expect to see God's escape route. Pharaoh has been looking for us all night, thinking that we had no place to go. Now he sees his slaves escaping. Pharaoh's easy victory is quickly escaping him. So the battle cries are sounded. Pharaoh must move quickly, or lose his dominion over us forever.

The armies of Egypt prepare to chase after God's people. Yet in order to get us, our former master must cross the divide that separates the two different lands. Pharaoh owns the Sinai Peninsula, but Arabia is another matter; it is no man's land. Sure there are a few tribes to contend with, but there is no single force controlling the area. Pharaoh has no control of this land. Pharaoh and his armies must cross to Arabia if they are going to recapture us. The only problem is that for us to cross over to the wilderness, we have to die. After we die, we were raised with Christ. We encounter the cross of Christ and His death under the waterline of the sea. Something in us dies while the new life of God raises us into a new relationship with Him in a new land. Now, as we watch from the other shore, evil is trying to follow that same path in order to get to us. The path it is following, however, was not designed for it.

When evil steps into the sea and attempts to follow the path God designed for His people, it encounters the cross just as we do. The difference is plain. At the cross, evil encounters death and is not resurrected. When evil encounters the death of the cross, it is finished. Evil will not be able to enter the wilderness because it can not enter the life of God; it dies before our eyes! We watch as evil attempts to follow our path and drowns.

The evil in our lives becomes a postscript in our history. Evil is completely removed from us so that we will never be tempted by it again, nor bow to its control. We will never pay the price for having a relationship with that evil again. We are now living in freedom on the other side of the sea. After encountering the cross, we came up in a new life. Finally, we feel free, look free and are beginning to act free.

God's people have often forgotten about living in the life of God. They replace the life of God with their own religious traditions, settling for man-made rules. By so doing, they miss the vibrancy God designed for us to be living in. God's traditions will bring life, while our traditions make null God's word. Throughout Scripture we find only one thing that has the ability to thwart God's word: the traditions of man. When freedom comes, the reality of a personal relationship with a living God becomes the norm for every day. We cannot deny Him or His sovereignty in our lives. If we ever question our relationship with God, all we need to do is look up! It is when we attempt to replace this relationship that we get into trouble.

It is easy for us to live at the cross, to continually beat ourselves up. Granted, a part of us must stay at the cross at all times. Our flesh (that part of us that stands against the ways of God) must remain dead and become a permanent fixture of Calvary. The events of the cross must never be minimized. The gift of God at the cross must never be slighted. The sacrifice of the Lord at the cross must never be underestimated. Yet there will be no life or fulfillment in God unless we come out of the water. We must find the Lord after His resurrection and live in

His life! We must tie ourselves to the life of God and settle for nothing less. Our goal in life should be like the Apostle Paul when he said,

> "That I may know Him, and the power of His resurrection, and the fellowship of His sufferings, being made conformable unto His death..." (Philippians 3:10)

Demons, angels, powers, and heavenly hosts will never know the rapture of being brought from death to life. There are certain paths in life that are only designed for us to travel. Only those of us who have come through the fire and the flood will be able to understand the full weight of the grace of God. There is a song to be sung that can only be expressed by the redeemed! Only those who know redemption are able to sing the "Song of Moses!"

Father:
Redeem my life from destruction! Bring in Your life so that my life might have freedom. Bring me to death, that I might live! Conform me to Your death. I want Your Life. I need Your Life! As evil comes, I will trust You and hold my peace. I will not fear. Instead, I will watch Your hand move on my behalf. Come quickly Lord and have Your way!

CHAPTER 7

Praise

Passover Cup #4

Then sang Moses and the children of Israel this song unto the LORD, and spake, saying, I will sing unto the LORD, for He hath triumphed gloriously: the horse and his rider hath He thrown into the sea. The LORD is my strength and song, and He is become my salvation: he is my God, and I will prepare Hm an habitation; my father's God, and I will exalt Him. The LORD is a man of war: the LORD is His name. Pharaoh's chariots and his host hath he cast into the sea: his chosen captains also are drowned in the Red sea. The depths have covered them: they sank into the bottom as a stone. Thy right hand, O LORD, is become glorious in power: Thy right hand, O LORD, hath dashed in pieces the enemy. And in the greatness of Thine excellency Thou hast overthrown them that rose up against Thee: Thou sentest forth Thy wrath, which consumed them as stubble. And with the blast of Thy nostrils the waters were gathered together, the floods stood upright as an heap, and the depths were congealed in the heart of the sea. The enemy said, I will pursue, I will overtake, I will divide the spoil; my lust shall be satisfied upon them; I will draw my sword, my hand shall destroy them. Thou didst blow with Thy wind, the sea covered them: they sank as lead in the mighty waters. Who is like unto Thee, O LORD, among the gods? Who is like Thee, glorious in holiness, fearful in praises, doing wonders?   Exodus 15:1-11

> *And Miriam the prophetess, the sister of Aaron, took a timbrel in her hand; and all the women went out after her with timbrels and with dances. And Miriam answered them, Sing ye to the LORD, for He hath triumphed gloriously; the horse and his rider hath He thrown into the sea. Exodus 15:20-21*

We have just witnessed the destruction of evil. The enemy that held us bound has been defeated before our eyes. We have seen first hand the greatness of our God, and a deathblow against Pharaoh and his army. That evil will never trouble us again! The power that held us captive is gone forever and we will never have to fight that trouble again! The evil, which called us its slave, is permanently removed from our lives.

Pharaoh and his armies could not follow the path of death and survive. We thought for certain that Pharaoh would destroy us in the desert and our lives would end. And the truth is, we were right! This day we died. Yet the death we experienced was not what we were expecting. Our very death in the Red Sea brought us life! Today our enemy was destroyed. Pharaoh's death has brought our freedom.

We are now completely and totally owned by God Himself. Our complete source of life is now the God of all creation. The path made possible by our Savior has brought us back to a relationship with God our Father. On the night our Lord was betrayed, He said it this way: "In my Father's house are many mansions... I go to prepare a place for you!" (John 14:2) Who would have thought it possible? God has made a place for us in Himself! Eden has been restored. The effects of sin have been overturned. The relationship with God, lost by Adam and Eve, has been restored to us by the completed work of Jesus Christ. We have been redeemed. Our ownership has been transferred eternally to our God. We can never be taken away from Him again!

How do we respond to this newly found freedom in our relationship with God? We jump to our feet, not really caring who is watching. We're not interested what people may think. Nothing can hold us down or prevent us from letting our feelings be known to all around.

Chapter 7

The joy can't be contained. We shout, dance, sing, and grab each other by the hand as the music starts and everybody takes their place. The timbrels come out, for the voice alone will not suffice to express the greatness of our God. The praise begins. It cannot be stopped - it must come! No one has to organize it or attempt to define it. In fact, it can't be defined, nor can this kind of praise be planned; it just erupts. On this day there is no way that praise can be prevented. The excitement can't be contained, nor the joy held in. Neither can the newly found freedom be downplayed. We can't be quiet! Everything within us is demanding the exaltation of our King. Today our God will be praised, and we will do it! The rocks will hold their peace, for today we have been set free. Everyone around us is going to know how this new freedom has come. We will praise the Lord!

The freedom we now are experiencing brings a euphoria we weren't expecting. Prior to this, we had no idea why we were so weighted down. Just a few moments ago we were staring death in the face. There appeared to be no hope, but now we are free, and the death that tried to take us is dead. We were burdened, but now we feel light, being freed from our previous weights so that we now want to jump into the heavens. Only gravity is preventing us from leaving the bounds of earth. We are so excited that we have to move around and dance! Who could have imagined or grasped the magnitude of our salvation, and comprehended what God had prepared for us?

We have seen the saving hand of God, the freeing touch of our Lord. So we begin to sing a new song. It is new to us; we would not have understood it before. We now sing in freedom a new and unique song of what we have just witnessed. We are telling the story of what God has just done, being completely consumed by His greatness.

We sing a song that can only be sung by those redeemed by the blood of the Lamb. No other creature can understand the words we use or the enthusiasm with which we sing. Only those who have seen and experienced the wondrous salvation of our God can sing this song. We have seen His salvation and witnessed God's outstretched arms bringing us back to Himself. Wondrous, miraculous, amazing, and awesome barely describes what we have just seen. So we declare to each other that we will sing unto our God, for He has triumphed gloriously. We look at each other in amazement and ask one another if everyone just saw what had happened.

God's glory has been made known to mankind. Heaven has moved into the affairs of earth. God has revealed His majesty to His people. God is real. He really loves me! He has cared enough to change my life! The result of seeing the glory of God in our lives sends us to praise. We praise our God who has thrown the horse and rider into the sea, and has delivered us from evil.

We sing to each other. We sing to all that can hear, to the heavens, and to the earth. As our feet move underneath us, we sing and dance. We let all creation and all of heaven know that our Redeemer lives. We sing the song of the redeemed declaring that our Redeemer lives. We sing of the mighty works of our God as well as His greatness. We sing of His marvelous deeds towards us; of His total defeat of our enemy who thought he would keep us in slavery. We sing of those bought with a price and freed to the wondrous care of a living God. We lift up the name of our God from whom all blessings flow. We praise God for what He has done!

The sense to praise is so strong that if we try to hold back, we will burst. If we do hold back the rocks around us will be forced to cry out in song and lift up the majestic name of our great King! Today, no one will praise for us. We will sing the praises of our God until all of creation joins us in singing. Prior to this point, we had no idea what God was doing or why. We didn't understand what freedom or redemption might mean. We couldn't comprehend the meaning of the actions God had directed us to take, which allowed our enemy to threaten us one last time. But now we see the wisdom of God! We understand God's plan for us to this point; why He took us out of Egypt and allowed us to be backed up at the Red Sea. We see the wonders of God's redemption and marvel at His greatness. Now His majesty must be declared, and His goodness towards mankind sounded to all who will listen. We shout so that all will hear, "He who has an ear, let him hear!"

CHAPTER 7

Praise Belongs to the Free

Praise must follow redemption. When we are bought back and evil has been dealt the deathblow, praise must come! In fact, if praise doesn't follow there never was redemption. What we call deliverance turns out to be nothing more than a sham, if true heartfelt praise doesn't erupt. Praise belongs to the free. It is reserved to those who are redeemed by the blood of the Lamb. The ability to praise is the unique characteristic of those set free by God!

Any being in heaven or on earth can worship God by simply acknowledging who He is. In fact, you don't even have to be saved to worship God. After all, even the demons acknowledge who God is and yield to His sovereignty. Praise, though, belongs to the redeemed. Only those bought with a price can praise the Lord for what He has done in their lives! When someone has been freed they will break out in praise; it is as simple as that. Without such praise you can be certain that God has not touched a person. If you have witnessed God bringing freedom to a life you will know it was real when you hear the praises of our God rolling off the tongue of the person being freed. Their appearance changes, as God makes the crooked paths straight. There will be no doubt in your mind that you have witnessed the miraculous and sovereign hand of God set a person free, claim that life as His own. You may have played a part in the deliverance, but you know that the life you see came from God Himself.

Praise belongs to the free, to those who have been saved. Those who have seen the hand of God move in their lives, who know the sovereign leading of the Lord, cannot help but sing praise. And yet, everyone who claims the name of Jesus Christ has at least one mighty act for which to praise God: deliverance from the kingdom of darkness to the kingdom of God. We all should be able to shout the praises of our God for bringing us to rebirth. Each person in the body of Christ should be able to praise God for what He has done.

So, we praise God for His marvelous works towards men. "Oh, that men would give thanks to the Lord!" (Psalm 107:8). That is our cry when we see the redemption of our God. We begin to wonder why everyone else doesn't see what we see. We wonder why all people aren't joining in the song. We honestly desire for everyone to live in the freedom we are now enjoying. We want everyone to have this relationship with our God.

We declare God's complete ownership of our lives, that He is the Lord our God, the Sovereign One. Oh, how we now trust the One Who directs our paths! He is Lord of all and is to be obeyed - my personal God who has joined Himself to me. He is my God and there is none like Him. I will bow the knee to no other god. He is mine and I am His. From now on, we will walk together as one. Nothing in heaven or on earth will be able to separate me from Him. I have seen His hand move on my behalf, and I will never again allow the doubt of His love to overtake me. I will trust Him and love Him. I will walk with Him alone from now on!

As we sing our new song we begin to understand our complete dependence on God. We begin to realize that He is our total source for everything. God truly is our strength and song. He is the reason for our song. It is all about Him and His goodness. It is all about Him and His love for me. He is our reason for being, our health and our strength. He is the song we sing.

Exodus 15:2 shows the exciting result from our praise:

> *"The LORD is my strength and song, and He is become my salvation: he is my God, and I will prepare Him an habitation; my father's God, and I will exalt Him."*

The word habitation is often translated praise. In reality, when we praise God for what He has done we are adorning, beautifying, and preparing a home for God to dwell in. Our praises literally decorate a place for God to inhabit. Every time we sing of the mighty works of our Lord we add decoration to the place where He lives. We adorn a home fit for a King! It is a home that is dramatically different than the home we left behind in Egypt. Yet life itself is so different now.

CHAPTER 7

After we have been redeemed we feel complete. Even though our redemption has just occurred, we know the dramatic change has revolutionized our life and existence. From now on, nothing will be the same. We know we will never see Pharaoh again. The evil that consumed us is dead.

The question is, "Does God really bring that kind of freedom today?" So often, a person will kick himself or herself for having waited so long to trust God and turn to Him, realizing what they have missed. People often act as though they had a choice in God's timing. Or else they blame others around them for not forcing them into the will of God sooner. Yet now they are free and it feels good! God's work in the Spirit has invaded the realm of the emotions and it overflows to all around. For the first time, God has control of an area of their life previously held captive, and all seems right.

If you are not living in the freedom of God, know today that God's life is available to you also. You can sing the song of the redeemed! You too can sing, shout, dance, and be overwhelmed by the greatness, holiness, and glory of our living God. You can come under the authority of the Lord Jesus Christ and watch the evil in your life dealt the deathblow, as you trust God to bring the effects of redemption into your life. Yes! You can be free, saved, and redeemed! The freedom of praise can be yours as well. You can join the countless numbers who will be standing in heaven, by the sea of crystal, declaring the power and might of our great King!

True joy and happiness is found only in the presence of the Lord. Today, let each of us purpose in our hearts to join God where He is. Let each of us purpose that we will not settle for second best. We will seek after the One who can give us life. May each of us know the freedom to sing the song of the redeemed!

The Praise of the Ages

Moses, David, and Deborah are among those biblical characters who have exampled the pure song of praise. They saw the hand of God move in the affairs of man, taking what was wrong and making it right.

They watched God take that which was outside His will and ways, and bring righteousness. They witnessed God bringing people back to a proper standing and relationship with Him. When God was finished, they understood what He had done and why. The result was a pure song of praise. The result was the song of Moses, a song that will be sung again as God's plans continue to be revealed.

The song of praise has been, and always will be, sung with understanding. When a pure song of praise is lifted to God we understand why God brought us through what He did. We understand the big picture. The result is complete and total amazement. We never would have imagined that the actions God took (and asked us to take) would bring the freedom we now enjoy. We could not have conceived a plan similar to what God designed for us. In fact, if we had known of God's plan we probably would have run away in fear. We now understand (at least, in part) that God's ways are beyond our comprehension. We never could have planned a scheme to completely humiliate evil the way God has done. Yet that is how God has been defeating evil from the beginning.

Throughout history we see God using evil to bring its own defeat and to bring His people freedom. Evil, in all its arrogance, stands up in defiance to God. Yet the destruction of evil is always close at hand. Evil will not be tolerated in God's domain. It will not be allowed to exist indefinitely in God's creation. Pride and arrogance will fall. Nothing (and no one) will ever share the glory reserved for God on His throne. Evil will fall and pride will be humiliated. Arrogance will see defeat.

The destruction of evil is always imminent. During the time the Lord walked on the earth, evil had no idea how its destruction was at hand. Evil had no idea that it would bring about its own destruction. All evil saw was the Son of God walking on earth in a human body. It realized the danger of God ruling as a human being and set its sights on destroying His human body. Evil believed that destroying the body of the Lord would remove the immediate problem; after all, how can he rule as a human being if He has no body? The plan of evil should have worked. Evil tried to destroy the Lord as a child and failed. Later, when the Lord was given the power of the Holy Spirit, evil attempted to separate Him

CHAPTER 7

from the power of heaven. Finally, after thirty-three years of trying evil was able to destroy his Body.

Evil thought the job was finished, and the problem was solved. Little did it realize that its problems were just beginning! In reality, evil's success in killing the Lord was its complete failure. By killing the Lord, evil sent the Son of God back to heavenly realm. All of evil's work through the ages, including the undoing of Eden, had just been destroyed. Evil thought it had gotten rid of the authority of God on earth. What evil received instead was the authority of God spread throughout the planet in countless people, empowered by God Himself with the Spirit of His Son. Once again, evil had been duped into bringing about its own destruction. In addition, evil's plan to prevent God ruling on earth in human form was thwarted by the Lord's resurrection. Not only could mankind now be restored to a relationship with God and rule on earth, God now had the legal right to rule as a man as well. The Lord's body was not destroyed, it did not see corruption. Jesus could still rule as a human being! Evil was completely ruined!

While this pattern of destroying evil has been true throughout the course of history, the truth remains constant and with us today. God is using the same means in each of our lives. Every knee that bows before Him will see the salvation of our God in their lives and the destruction of evil. This truth will continue as history, itself, is brought to a close, as well. We will see the finished work of the Lord at Calvary continue to ripple throughout time, until all evil has been removed from God's creation. Like a heavy stone thrown into a calm pond, the effects of the Lord's work will reach the shores as He sits at the right hand of the Father.

Today, God is using the Body of Christ to bring that destruction. Yes, today we are playing an active role in the destruction of evil. Three things associated with the Body of Christ will ultimately overcome evil: the word of our testimony, the blood of the Lamb, and not loving our lives even to death. (Revelation 12:11) As we live our lives, our actions are bringing a continuing defeat to the forces of evil. The effects of sin are being undone. The restoration of people to a proper relationship with God is continuing. The dominion of God is being re-established on the earth as His kingdom is advanced.

Until the day of the total annihilation of evil, creation itself will continue to groan as it waits for the sons of God to be revealed. We also wait for the glory of God to be made physically evident on this planet. We long for the return of the Lord. We long for Him to set all things right as we earnestly wait for the creation of a new heaven and earth. We can't wait for the destruction of the final evil, which is death.

Just as evil was duped into bringing freedom to Israel, and was duped into bringing our freedom on the cross, evil will be duped into ushering in the physical reign of Christ on this planet. God's plan of redemption will continue for mankind as evil makes its next mistake; and this mistake will be a big one. It will again result in the releasing of stolen authority. The Messiah will be revealed as the millennial rule of the Lord begins. The Lord will reign, not the forces of evil. It will be the time of the honeymoon for a newly married Bride and Groom, a thousand years of peace and celebration. After this time, evil will be duped once again and will attempt to attack the Lord Himself. The result of this blunder will usher in the creation of a new heaven and new earth where God the Father will physically live with His people.

The redemption of the cross and empty tomb is not only bringing life to people, but life back to the creation itself. The redemption of mankind is still unfolding before us. God's plan for the destruction of evil is still unfolding before us, and we have the opportunity to play a role. The work of the Lord as He lived, died, and rose again is continuing today after two thousand years, and we have the awesome privilege of witnessing all enemies of the Lord being placed under His feet.

Someday (and may it be soon) there will not be anything on earth outside the will and ways of God. Someday there will be no trouble or problems. God's plan for the total destruction of evil will have been accomplished. All things will have been set right, so that there will be no more heartache, suffering, or pain. All will be well in the dominion of our God. God Himself will live with His people and wipe away every tear. Everyone will know God and be in relationship with Him.

There will come a day when all the redeemed of the earth will be in together, in the physical presence of God, waiting for one of our own to say the words we all have been longing to hear. Those words sounded will stop all activity in heaven, and every creature will understand the ramifications of what is about to occur. The voice will cry out, "Praise our God, all ye His servants, and ye that fear Him, both small and great!" (Revelation 19:5) When these words are sounded all will know that the redemption of mankind is complete and it is time for praise to erupt. Those words will signal that the time has come for the Bride of Christ to take her place and that the marriage of the Lamb of God has come. The final cup of the Passover will be raised, the Cup of Praise. That cup will be taken together under the canopy of the covering of God as Husband and Wife. This cup has been reserved since our Lord's time on earth. On the night of the Last Supper, the Lord said, "I will not drink henceforth of this fruit of the vine, until that day when I drink it new with you in my Father's kingdom!" (Matthew 26:29) What a day! Pure praise will sound throughout all of heaven as the Groom and His Bride are married.

The response to the cry from heaven will be from all the redeemed of the earth. Every voice that has known the salvation, deliverance, and freedom of our God will respond in one voice, "Alleluia: for the Lord God omnipotent reigneth!" A pure song of praise will sound throughout the heavenlies from the redeemed of the earth. A pure song of praise will exalt the wonders of our God. The marriage of the Bride has come, and she has made herself ready. The Bride has prepared herself to be married, and the Cup of Praise will usher in her marriage. During her preparation, she learned how to be a wife and love her husband. For the first time ever, the true Proverbs thirty-one woman is revealed as praise explodes.

Today, any praise that we lift up to the heavens is mere dress rehearsal for this awesome day. When we gather with the body of Christ, we are simply practicing for that day when we will sing the song of the redeemed!

At the time of the wedding feast, we will then understand why God took the paths He did to redeem the earth. We will understand why He chose Israel and gave them the Torah. We will understand why sin ruled for a time, as well as the true power of the resurrection of the Lord. We will see clearly why God entrusted the Church with His authority, and why it seemed so long for the Lord's return. We will understand it all. When we do understand it, praise will erupt. No one in heaven will be able to hold back the praise. We will sing, dance, and shout as we tell each other of the wonder of our God. The redeemed of the earth will sound their song of pure praise as the song of Moses permeates heaven itself.

The sea of the redeemed will stand before God Himself, a sea like crystal. The song will be sung, the song that only the redeemed of the earth can understand. Only those who have seen the deliverance, redemption, and salvation of their God can join the song. Only those who have been set free can understand the meaning of the verses sung. It will be sung in purity, as a wedding celebration that will last one thousand years begins. It will be a time of peace designed as a honeymoon for the Groom and His Bride, a time that will not end until God Himself is ready to reveal the glory of a new heaven and new earth, where He will live with His people. It will be a time when we begin to see the indescribable things God has prepared for His people.

Lord:

We declare that You are great and marvelous! Your deeds are beyond measure! You have triumphed gloriously! You have redeemed our lives from destruction! We exalt You as Sovereign Lord! Come now Lord and take Your place with Your people. Let us begin our life of freedom together! Join Yourself to us that we may be one!

CHAPTER 8

Welcome to the Wilderness

We have been purified, delivered, and redeemed. Our praise to God has sounded to all who can hear. We have a new relationship with the God of all creation. God Himself is personally directing our path and has taken intimate control of our lives. Have we arrived? Is this all that there is? Where do we go from here? Are we in the Promised Land?

All too often, after God has radically changed a person, we think this is the end of the rainbow and that they are ready to go into their Promised Land. We often encourage them to conquer the Promised Land as soon as they have crossed the Red Sea. We treat them as though they have arrived. This seems to make sense, since the sovereign hand of God is clearly visible in that person's life. When we, personally, come through the Red Sea, we are eager to inhabit our own land. We long to cross the Jordan River and take what is ours. After all, the Jordan River is nothing compared to the Red Sea. Our faith is riding high and we feel like we can conquer anything. We are ready for the fight. Yet that is not God's way.

Too often, I have seen hands laid on people much too quickly with devastating results. The Scriptures give numerous examples of those who attempted to take their place before their time. The results were always the same—trouble was found on all fronts. Even the Apostle Paul could not rush into ministry before God's time. When people enter battles too soon, blood is often spilled and people get hurt. Frustration, burnout, lack of vision, and lack of leadership can often be the result of people jumping the gun prior to God's release. They may have a destiny and a calling to fulfill, yet God's timing is everything.

People often miss the lessons and excitement of the wilderness. The most common result of sidestepping the wilderness is a lack of submission. Today, far too many Christians lack the ability to submit to others and to authority, having never been trained by God. They are used to doing things for themselves and have never learned the lessons of the wilderness. The result is, they become loose cannons, causing problems instead of bringing the solutions.

We are often so eager to take our place within the Body of Christ that we forget to first learn how to fight. We often find people in leadership positions within the church who are completely unprepared to lead. The reason is simple: they have skipped the wilderness. We have too many churches losing ground today because they have disregarded the vital lessons of the wilderness. When people skip the wilderness, they end up living with a slave mentality. It is a mentality that costs dearly, preventing them from coming into full ownership of what God has prepared.

We want to run to the Promised Land. However, God has other things in mind for us. The Promised Land is nowhere in sight. In fact, there will not be an opportunity to enter our own place for over two years. So where are we? And what are we doing here?

Welcome to the wilderness! The wilderness? Yes, that's right! We have just been released from bondage and plopped into the wilderness. We are finally finished with slavery and look where we are! No one would have believed that we have come so far just to rot in the desert. "God, You've got to be kidding!"

But, it's no joke. God has us in the desert, in a dry, barren land for a very good reason: it is time to undo the ways of sin, replacing them with God's ways. In Egypt, we learned how to live our lives as slaves to Pharaoh. Our habits and patterns for life were based on our slave lifestyle. Now it is time to learn God's way for us to live. In order for us to be able to conquer the land and take our place we will need to relearn how to live. The old ways of conducting ourselves will not work against giants. It is time to learn how to think and live as God originally designed. We will have no chance of winning and holding our land without change taking place. Crossing the Jordan River will be pointless until we learn how to live under the direction and sovereignty of God. It is time to learn obedience and faith, replacing a slavery mentality with a godly mentality!

Pharaoh and his armies lie dead behind us. Before us, the desert looms as the glory of God leads. Who knows where the pillar will lead us or what we will encounter? Does God understand all of our needs? How will we eat and where will we get water to drink? Yet the pillar has us on the move, and our time of schooling has begun.

We often view the wilderness as a rotten place to be. While the desert can certainly be a scary place, it provides an opportunity for us to spend time alone with God. In the wilderness, God is not only training us, He has drawn close so that we can see and hear His every move. The wilderness is an intimate time, a time where it is just God and us. The wilderness is a time where God is supernaturally teaching us His mind and ways. In the desert, God reveals who He really is. Our part is simply to learn, obey, and not fear. God is fully in control in the wilderness, and we will see things we never could have imagined; things our children will talk about for years to come. They will revolutionize our way of thinking and how we conduct ourselves. Here in the wilderness, our old patterns are going to be ripped out of us and be replaced with patterns of living, fit for a prince or princess. We will learn how to conduct ourselves as royalty. We are going to get a crash course in proper human behavior.

Israel would spend the next two years in the desert preparing to enter the Promised Land. After the initial two years of traveling, God led them to the border of their land. He fully expected them to cross over.

Israel's unbelief cost them forty years of traveling time that included twenty-eight different stops. The first two-year period in the wilderness was their training period. During this time, God led them to twelve specific places; twelve stops that number God's complete government. At each of these spots, God brought a specific lesson to be learned; a visual lesson that would change their lives forever.

Marah

Exodus 15:23-26

Welcome to Marah! You are so thirsty that you can hardly stand it. In front of you is a water hole, to which you run with the rest of the people for a drink. You stoop over and take a drink, yet as soon as the water is in your mouth you spit it out. It is so bitter you can't drink it. There is no other water in sight. You are in the middle of the desert without any prospects of finding any relief for your thirst. So what do you do? You complain to Moses, who passes on your complaint to God, who responds with strange instructions. The next thing you see is a tree being thrown into the water. How is this supposed to help? Even though it doesn't make sense, people are now drinking the water. You try the water again and this time it is sweet. You don't understand it. How could one tree affect enough water to quench the thirst of over two million people? Yet the water tastes great. Your thirst is quenched. A miracle has just taken place before your eyes, and you will never forget it!

With this picture fresh in Israel's mind, God then gives them their first lesson:

> *"If you will diligently hearken to the voice of the Lord your*
> *God and do that which is right in His eyes, and give heed to*
> *His commandments and keep all His statutes, I will put*

> *none of the diseases upon you which I put upon the Egyptians; for I am the Lord your healer." Exodus 15:26*

With the visible reminder of the bitter water being turned sweet, the words just spoken take on fresh meaning. No one will ever forget this lesson. If I obey, I will be spared the price of sin and won't have the problems other people have. Bitterness will be turned to sweetness before my eyes. God will make the disgusting palatable. If I don't obey, however, God won't remove the bitterness and my thirst will never be quenched!

Imagine a tree bringing life: a tree thrown into death bringing a sweet satisfaction to your thirst! That which was bitter and not palatable is now made drinkable by sacrificing a tree.

> *"...he that believeth on Me shall never thirst." (John 6:35)*

From Elim to the Wilderness of Sin
Exodus 15:27 – 16:36

Israel's next two and a half months are a rush to Mount Sinai. God kept the two million, or so, Israelites on the move constantly. Six stops awaited Israel as they left Marah: Elim, the Red Sea, the Wilderness of Sin, Dophkah, Alush, and Rephidim. From Marah, God brings His people to Elim, a place of rest. At Elim, Israel rests among twelve fountains of water and seventy palm trees. From Elim, God takes Israel back to the Red Sea. Now this must have been a test of patience for Israel. It must have seemed like they were going in circles. Yet the people held their peace.

Leaving the Red Sea, Israel is led by the pillars to the Wilderness of Sin (Sin in this case means "thorn or clay"). It is here, in the

Wilderness of Sin, that Israel learns its next major lesson. Once again, obedience is the theme.

In the Wilderness of Sin, Israel grew hungry. They began to murmur to each other and complain to Moses. You would think that they should have learned about complaining, already having possessed enough faith to trust God. Yet trusting God went right out the window as soon as their bellies began to growl. Interestingly, God doesn't punish them for their complaining. Later on, in their journey they would try the same thing again and pay the price. But for now, God let their lack of trust go. In fact, once again He gave Israel the food they wanted, although what He provided wasn't exactly what the people were looking for. They were given a special food that required special handling to be eaten. God gave Israel manna.

In addition to the manna, Israel got a onetime dose of quail meat as well. However, the gift of manna would become their steady diet for the next forty-two years. The people would have to work for the manna, following a specific set of guidelines for its collection and storage. Gathering and eating food may seem rather basic and mundane, yet God had a very good reason for this structure. He wanted to prove whether or not the people would walk in His law. The daily eating habits themselves would demonstrate to Israel their need to obey God and follow Him. In Marah, they learned the importance of obeying God. Now in the Wilderness of Sin, they would be forced to obey or starve. The simple task of gathering food would prove whether or not Israel could obey and follow instructions.

The lessons Israel learned in the Wilderness of Sin are still a part of our own training process today. He who is faithful in little will be given much. God starts us out with the basics, and our tasks are usually physical. He may ask us to clean the toilets at church, paint a shut-in's house, join a work party, buy a person some gas for their car, take someone to the laundromat, or cook a meal for a new mother. While the tasks may seem mundane, God is teaching us faithfulness and how to obey. He is proving whether or not we will follow Him. The Apostle Paul shed light on this reality when he told Timothy,

CHAPTER 8

> *"And the things that thou hast heard of me among many witnesses, the same commit thou to faithful men, who shall be able to teach others also."* (2 Timothy 2:2)

The command to Timothy was to train faithful men. Timothy was to disciple faithful men who could be trusted to pass on what they had learned to others. Before real training can begin, faithfulness must be developed. A person must first be trained in integrity before spiritual realities are entrusted to him. A person who cannot prove his faithfulness in small things will never be given greater assignments. As a result, within the church today much of our efforts are geared towards teaching faithfulness and integrity. As soon as a person can be proven faithful, their real training can begin.

From Dophkah to Rephidim
Exodus 17:1 – 18:27

Israel continued their journey from the Wilderness of Sin to Dophkah. From Dophkah, they traveled to Alush and from Alush they went to Rephidim. This was a whirlwind tour, God leading them through all three areas in less than two weeks. Mount Sinai was next on God's itinerary. Before Israel was ready for the lessons of Mount Sinai, though, specific preparations were needed for which Rephidim was key. Discipline and organization of the people were lessons to learn quickly. Without it, Israel's leadership would soon burn out and become ineffective. In Rephidim, three life-changing events would take place that would be remembered throughout the remainder of human history.

Israel had been on the move from Egypt for less than three months. Within this short period of time, they had witnessed the miraculous and the impossible. Every norm had been challenged and every concept of God redrawn. Yet here at Rephidim, the basic need for water caused the people to question God's provision. Once again they were thirsty. So they complained to Moses, rather than trust God to meet their need. The response of Moses was amazing. Why do you contend with me? Why are you angry with me? What have I to do with the problem? You can see the frustration in Moses. He is merely following God's instruction; he certainly didn't want the responsibility of leading a nation. Yet there he was between an irate group of thirsty people and God, and his leadership skills were maxed out. Moses didn't have a solution for the mob that was ready to stone him.

God gave Moses instructions that would miraculously provide water for the thirsty people of Israel. The immediate need would be met. Yet the growing problem in the heart of Moses had been exposed. He was tired of carrying the burden alone. In fact, he could not carry the burden anymore. He was running out of personal resources, and without change, it was unlikely he would be able to go on. He was paying a high cost for leading Israel and the toll was beginning to show. It was time for the people to step up and share the load. And that is exactly what God wanted Israel to learn to do.

Shortly after the incident with the water, Amalek attacked at Rephidim. The newly created army of Israel was about to see action for the first time. Yet this would not be a conventional battle. Israel would be victorious only as long as God's instructions to Moses were carefully followed. While the men fought, Moses went up a nearby hill and held up his shepherd's rod in the air with both arms. As long as his hands remained in the air Israel gained, but when his hands fell they lost. Needless to say it didn't take the people around Moses long to figure out that they needed to come along side of Moses in order to hold up his arms. It didn't take a lot of thought, but was in their best interest to hold up the arms of God's leadership!

Shortly after the battle with Amalek, Moses received a visit from his father-in-law, Jethro. As he watched the manner in which Moses led Israel, he challenged him to spread out the responsibilities. These three things: Moses' frustration in leadership, God's lesson with Amalek, and the challenge of Jethro came together to change the destiny of Israel. Moses would have to release some of the load, so that the people would step forward and take their place. For Israel to proceed on this journey, leadership would have to change and the people start taking responsibility for themselves. The complaining to Moses would have to end. The people needed to grow up. The physical, administrative burden of being a family and a people needed to be shared.

The lesson of Rephidim is still an important lesson today. If any group within the body of Christ is going to see success, the people must take their place. The body of Christ was never designed to be a one-leader show. Every person is vitally needed for God's plan of success to be realized. No part is greater than another but every part is needed. In addition, people must begin to realize that it is in their own best interest to hold up the arms of leadership and fight the battles. Leaders must understand that God has designed the burdens to be shared with all the people.

Mount Sinai
Exodus 19:1 – 40:38

Three months after leaving Egypt, Israel found themselves at their seventh stop, the foot of Mount Sinai. They would spend the next two years learning the most important lessons God had for them. Here at Mount Sinai Israel would learn how to relate to God Himself as His beloved children. The covenant would be renewed and the teachings (Torah) would be given. The Tabernacle would also be given and the Levites set apart. Israel would be organized into families (or tribes) and these families would learn how to relate to each other. Together the tribes would relate to God, each one serving a specific function within the whole. Eventually, each tribe would conquer the land and be designated a specific piece of it.

Israel could not deny that God had brought them to Mount Sinai, or that God Himself was taking charge of the next two years. Israel wanted to see God (or at least they believed that they did), and God wanted them to know His greatness. Over the next two years, Israel saw enough of God to begin to understand His holiness and majesty. Thick clouds, thunder, lightning, fire descending on the mountain, and earthquakes would reveal the sovereign nature of God to His people. By the time Israel's stop at Mount Sinai was over, they would understand that God was to be obeyed and trusted without question. He was the One who was to be worshiped as God alone, and loved as the Glorious One of Israel. From Mount Sinai afterwards, the people would have no excuse. They saw the wonders of God and He expected them to act accordingly. Hereafter, complaining was not to be tolerated, nor any challenges allowed to God's authority or the organization He put into place. From this point onward, the people of Israel would have a relationship with God like no other people on the planet, and God expected them to conduct themselves like it. A deeper relationship with God brought greater responsibility which in turn brought increased expectations. The people of Israel were growing up.

> *"...For unto whomsoever much is given, of him shall be much required..." (Luke 12:48)*

Growing up is a reality of life, both in the physical realm as well as the realm of the Spirit. As we grow in the Lord, He begins to expect proper behavior from us. Obedience is no longer and option. Childlike responses are no longer tolerated. Yet, our relationship with God is beyond explanation. The reality of God in our life is both close and undeniable! We begin to live in a relationship with God that was merely academic a short time ago.

From Taberah to Kadesh-barnea
Numbers 11:3, 11:34-35, 12:16, 33:16-18, Deuteronomy 1:1, 9:22

Once the command was given to leave Mount Sinai, the people of Israel were again on the move. They were headed towards the Promised Land and time was short. The most important lessons for conquering and holding the land had been learned over the last two years. The last

CHAPTER 8

four stops involved housekeeping details designed to reinforce to Israel that they were living under a different set of rules than when they left Egypt. The old ways would not succeed anymore, nor the old patterns be tolerated. The old slave mentality was a thing of the past. Self-centeredness could not be a part of conquering people. From Taberah to Kadesh-barnea some old lessons were revisited. This time however, God's response to the people was much different, as well as His expectation for the people. This time the people had no excuse.

After three days of journeying from Mount Sinai, Israel was at Taberah. Here God spread the spiritual responsibilities that Moses carried alone to seventy elders within the people. Earlier at Rephidim God had distributed the organizational authority. At Taberah the spiritual authority was distributed. In addition, the Israelites grasped a new understanding of their relationship to God. Prior to Mount Sinai they complained and got what they wanted. After Mount Sinai though, things were different. God's response was swift and fire consumed the complainers. They should have known better and trusted God, but they did not. As a result, many saw the judgment of God.

Israel journeyed a day from Taberah to Kibroth-hattaavah and complained again! This time they were hungry so God gave them food just as He had in the Wilderness of Sin. This time however, the food made them sick— in fact, it killed them! At Kibroth-hattaavah, Israel learned once and for all that trusting God was mandatory, not optional!

Hazaeroth was a short distance from Kibroth-hattaavah. It was here that politics took center stage. Aaron and Miriam attempted to remove Moses from power. Moses had married an Ethiopian woman and Aaron and Miriam believed that this disqualified him from leading Israel. The power struggle ended nearly as soon as it started. God intervened and Aaron and Miriam gained a new appreciation for Moses as the anointed of God. Aaron and Miriam's immediate disgrace taught everyone to respect God's anointed no matter what they may have thought of him! God's authority structure was not to be challenged.

The last stop prior to entering the Promised Land was Kadesh-barnea. From here, Israel was expected to conquer and hold their possessions.

They had been taught the lessons of the last two years and now it was time to put that knowledge and understanding to the test. Had they learned their lessons? Did they really have the understanding necessary to be conquerors? Did they truly trust God and love Him, so that they would fully obey Him? Would they be able to keep God as the central focus of their lives? These were the questions to be answered as soon as Israel left Kadesh-barnea. Yet even though God said they were ready, the people of Israel had a different idea.

Spies were sent into the land of Canaan with all, but two, returning with reports of fear and defeat. Though they should have known better, the people buckled under the bad reports. Their lack of trust in God at this point cost them their inheritance in the Promised Land. Why? Because of unbelief! They should have trusted God and His direction for their lives, yet they still would not believe.

The lesson this generation of Israelites must learn is harsh! Once the training of the people is completed God expects them to obey and take the land. The meaning of this is clear. God expects His people to become productive in His kingdom. The Israelites who refused to trust God and take their place, paid dearly. Judgment was swift and irreversible and they were banished back into the wilderness. Another generation would now enjoy what God had prepared for them, conquering the land and becoming a beacon to the rest of the world. Those who refused to let go of their slave mentality would be passed over for others. Those who had been freed, redeemed and trained would be left to finish out their days without realizing their destiny. Someone else would enjoy the benefits of their destiny!

God had brought Israel out of the land of slavery and bondage. He had purified, delivered, and redeemed the people. He took them on a journey through the wilderness that lasted just over two years, bringing them into a new relationship with their Creator and their God. They were given every opportunity in the wilderness to replace their slavery mentality with a godly mentality; to take God's mind, thought, and emotions and make them their own.

After this incredible journey from bondage to freedom and beyond,

CHAPTER 8

God had destined for them to live a life they could not have understood. God had prepared for them a place to live and rule, a place from which the glory of God would touch the ends of the earth. Called by His name, God's people would be a sign and a seal to all other peoples on the planet. Israel was literally an expression of God's rule and character on earth which all could see and be drawn to. Israel's destiny would reveal the pattern of God's salvation for all generations to come, a pattern that would be repeated fifteen hundred years later on a hill just north of the temple, on an old rugged cross!

What was the wilderness like for Israel? It was a place that tested and tried everything that they believed. The wilderness transformed their idea of what a god really was. It was here that Israel came to know the true God. He was not a silent rock or tree, nor the sun, moon, or stars, aloof and untouchable. He was God and their very breath depended on Him.

The wilderness was stressful, yet it didn't have to be. Most fears and complaints could have been avoided if they had simply trusted God. If we also can learn this basic truth from the wilderness, our lives will become that much richer.

> "Trust in the LORD with all thine heart; and lean not unto thine own understanding. In all thy ways acknowledge Him, and He shall direct thy paths." (Proverbs 3:5-6)

If we travel the wilderness with the mentality that God can be trusted we find ourselves often saying, "So what." Are we hungry or thirsty? So what. Is Amalek coming? So what. Are we scared? So what. And the list goes on and on. Nothing can move or shake us, as we trust the Lord with all of our heart. What we feel, experience, live, and see means nothing compared to the word that God has spoken. "God is directing my paths! He can be trusted. Everything will work together for good!"

So it is God alone that matters. When we trust Him to lead us through the wilderness we leave there with our minds changed, ready to conquer a land before us. We will leave with testimonies of intimate times with our God, that future generations will recall. We will also come out of the wilderness with testimonies of a supernatural God who truly cares for His people.

Conclusion

Now freedom is complete. The mind of the slave has been transformed. Freedom could not exist without this transformation. Of course a person could live a life quasi-free with Pharaoh removed from their life. Yet as long as people lived like slaves, there would be no liberty. Nor would people find happiness who think and act in a self-centered manner. As long as people lived a self-centered life they would never gain the tools necessary to conquer the Promised Land!

With the mind, will and emotions transformed into the image of God a person can realize their potential and enjoy their destiny. The wilderness journey has prepared them to rule and represent the kingdom of God in their sphere of responsibility. Together with the rest of the body of Christ and with their families, a person can find a place of dominion and enjoy an inheritance given by God Himself. The body fights the larger battles, while the regional battles are fought as families. The local battles are fought by the soon to be landowner. Because of the process of salvation through Jesus the Christ a person can now conquer rather than be conquered, rule rather than be ruled.

Our destiny and our place are found in the Promised Land. People will never find their inheritance in Egypt or the wilderness. In addition, it is in the Promised Land that we find what our inheritance is about. We discover that our inheritance could not be taken without our freedom being declared and the lessons of the wilderness learned. Now, in the Promised Land, it is time to be productive. We can begin conquering the land that had been overrun with the ungodly and wild beasts. We begin to undo the years of ruin and neglect, building a future to be handed down to our children. We till, plant, and build so that an inheritance can be passed to those who will follow us. We remove the effects of sin from the land God has given to us, and make it a representation of God's rule and authority here on earth.

From God's act of delivering us from evil we can now enjoy a full life! As we yield aspects of our lives to Him, He takes the responsibility for us. There are no more worries or attempts at fixing things, nor wondering what to do or how to do it. Never again do we wonder how we fit in. God is in control and can be completely trusted.

God has given us all the precious gift of life. He has given every person who has come to Jesus a thrilling adventure to enjoy on this earth. We often forget that the Lord's burden is light. All too often we view our life on this earth as a dull drudgery to be relieved only by our death. However, God is not cruel! He wants us to enjoy our time on the earth. In addition, the journey He has prepared for us here is so much more than exciting. It is a journey that will not give us more than we can handle at one time. It continually brings freedom into our lives and places our dependence on God's goodness and sovereignty. It will not end for us until we finally shed these bodies that house us. God is preparing us to be married to the King!

God has prepared for each of us a journey to Him. It is a journey that never looks back, but continues to propel us upward. Today is always better than yesterday, but tomorrow will always be better than today. There will never be a look back at the "good old days." Our lives in God become an exciting time where we are brought from "faith to faith and glory to glory." Our faith is continually growing in Him. The glory of God is continually increasing in our lives. Everyday we see Him a little more clearly and walk just a little closer to Him. Everyday we learn to hear and follow Him a little better.

God's ways are so beyond our normal way of life. He really cares for us. He has designed for us a way of life that catapults us to living outside the normal human existence. The things that shake others around us do not affect us. For those of us living in God's ways, there are no bad days. Things may not always look good or right, yet we can endure cheerfully and hopefully. It becomes impossible not to be thankful for life. Death gives way to life. Our enemies become our best friends as they bring us ever closer to God. Tribulation is embraced because we know that God's grace is on the other side.

We live in the hope of seeing God's word accomplished in our lives. We learn as we travel to give thanks in all things because truly "all things work together for good to those who love Him." The goodness of God and His sovereign hand are a normal part of life. We are not surprised by the supernatural, but expect it because it is the norm for our lives! We begin to live in His grace and love, trusting that He can handle anything that comes our way. We are amazed by His love! His redeeming hand overwhelms us. We are enthralled with His majesty. We are eager for all of creation to join us in praising the name of our God.

The sovereign hand of God moves us continually closer to Him and transforms us into His image. He is continually transforming our mind, will, and emotions into the image of His Son. How God accomplishes this in us is exciting! God's process of leading us from "faith to faith" and "glory to glory" is truly an adventure to be anticipated with enthusiasm. Just when we think we have seen it all, God shows us something else. When we think we have arrived, God leads another part of us out of Egypt. Freedom is continually being brought into our lives and it increases every time another aspect of God's own nature is placed within us.

So enjoy your journey, child of the King! Enjoy what God has prepared for you. Cry out to your God and watch Him bring your freedom. Submit to His training and learn never to take a step without His leading. Take your place within the body of Christ and conquer the land before you. Know the peace and contentment that comes from living in your own place. And may He who is the Hope of all glory grow in your heart as God Delivers Us From Evil!

Come now Lord Jesus and lead Your church! Have Your way, Oh King Eternal! Father, Your ways are higher than our ways! You are worthy to be praised! Bring a pure song of praise to the lips

of Your people. Deliver us from evil! For Yours is the kingdom, and the power, and the glory forever!

  Amen!

www.ingramcontent.com/pod-product-compliance
Lightning Source LLC
LaVergne TN
LVHW041629070426
835507LV00008B/527